The MAILBOX
Bulletin Boards & Displays

grade **PreK**

Student-Centered Displays

- Reinforce key preschool learnings
- Showcase student work
- Help manage classroom routines
- Create a positive learning environment
- Help motivate students

Use throughout the year!

Managing Editor: Gerri Primak

Editorial Team: Becky S. Andrews, Kimberley Bruck, Sharon Murphy, Debra Liverman, Diane Badden, Thad H. McLaurin, Kimberly Brugger-Murphy, Brenda Miner, Kelly Robertson, Karen A. Brudnak, Jennifer Nunn, Hope Rodgers, Dorothy C. McKinney, Judy Aubuchon, Pam Ballingall, Cindy Barber, Dorothy Bickel, Susan Borland, Janet Boyce, Amy Brien, Susan Burbridge, Bobbi Chapman, Janet Christensen, Evalee Church, Kathy Clayton, Elizabeth Cook, Diane Crane, Jennifer Craven, Marcie Cup, Melissa Dean, Debbi Diperri, Candace Durinick, Marianne Edwards, Kris Evezic, Brenda Ferry, Susan Foulks, Louise Frankel, Joan Glaubitz-Morrison, Suzi Hart, Lucia Kemp Henry, Linda Herman, Jaima Hess, Sherry Hull, Camelia Kline, Laura Kopka, Sheryl Lammert, Shannon Lynch, Mary Martell, Shelly Mass, Eileen Massarotti, Tracie Maurer, Debra McConnell, Karen McGinley, Barb McWethy, Tracey Mikos, Stacy Milan, Janice Minton, Betsy Mohr, Wanda Monroe, Lil Morelli, Keely Peasner, Rebecca Perruquet, Gayle Piroli, Ginnie Postlethwaite, Susan Price, Marita Regier, Amy Reno, Sherri Rhyne, Mary Robles, Monica Sankey, Bobbi Schwartz, Bernice Sitkoff, Marti Stallknecht, Jill Stemple, Colleen Stephansen, Leanne Swinson, Christine Vohs, Dawn Waldron, Sharon Whitfield, Joyce Wilson, Yolanda Priscilla Zepeda

Production Team: Lori Z. Henry, Pam Crane, Rebecca Saunders, Chris Curry, Sarah Foreman, Theresa Lewis Goode, Greg D. Rieves, Eliseo De Jesus Santos II, Barry Slate, Donna K. Teal, Zane Williard, Tazmen Carlisle, Kathy Coop, Marsha Heim, Lynette Dickerson, Mark Rainey

www.themailbox.com

©2007 The Mailbox®
All rights reserved.
ISBN10 #1-56234-761-6 • ISBN13 #978-156234-761-1

Except as provided for herein, no part of this publication may be reproduced or transmitted in any form or by any means, electronic or mechanical, including photocopying, recording, or storing in any information storage and retrieval system or electronic online bulletin board, without prior written permission from The Education Center, Inc. Permission is given to the original purchaser to reproduce patterns and reproducibles for individual classroom use only and not for resale or distribution. Reproduction for an entire school or school system is prohibited. Please direct written inquiries to The Education Center, Inc., P.O. Box 9753, Greensboro, NC 27429-0753. The Education Center®, *The Mailbox*®, the mailbox/post/grass logo, and The Mailbox Book Company® are registered trademarks of The Education Center, Inc. All other brand or product names are trademarks or registered trademarks of their respective companies.

Manufactured in the United States
10 9 8 7 6 5 4 3 2 1

Table of Contents

Skills Grid 3

Quick Tips 4

Bulletin Boards and Displays

    Welcome to School 5

    Fall 15

    Winter 25

    Spring 39

    End of the Year 51

    Summer 55

    Anytime 61

        Curriculum 61

        Good Work 68

        Classroom Management 71

Patterns 74

Index 142

Pattern Index 144

Skills Grid

	Welcome to School 	Fall 	Winter 	Spring 	End of the Year 	Summer 	Anytime 
Creative Arts							
arts and crafts	8	18, 19, 23	26, 27, 28, 33, 35, 37, 38	40, 41, 42, 43, 46, 47, 49	52	56, 57, 58	63, 72
self-portraits	9						
Fine-Motor Skills							
coloring	6, 9		36				
crumpling			34, 37				
cutting			32	39, 49		57	
dipping				50			
gluing	10		27, 31, 32				
painting	7	22	29, 36		54		
printing			31	48			
rubbing			32				
weaving		15					
Listening and Speaking							
listening to clues							62
positional words				41, 45			
vocabulary development			28	48			
Literacy							
creative writing		24	30				
early writing		16	38	44, 48	51, 53		
letter recognition							64, 65
name recognition		20					
reading motivation		16					
rhyming			34				
Math							
comparing sets				45			67
counting	9	17, 24	30	44, 45		55	66, 67
matching							64, 67
picture graph						59	
puzzle							66
Science and Health							
dental health			36				
fire safety		19					
hygiene							63
plants				50			
pumpkins		20					
seasons		17	25				
Social Studies							
community							62
family		16, 22					
Martin Luther King Jr. Day			35				
Social and Emotional Development							
cooperation	8	21	29				61
self-concept	5, 6, 13				51, 54	60	
social relationships	9						
thankfulness		23					

Quick Tips

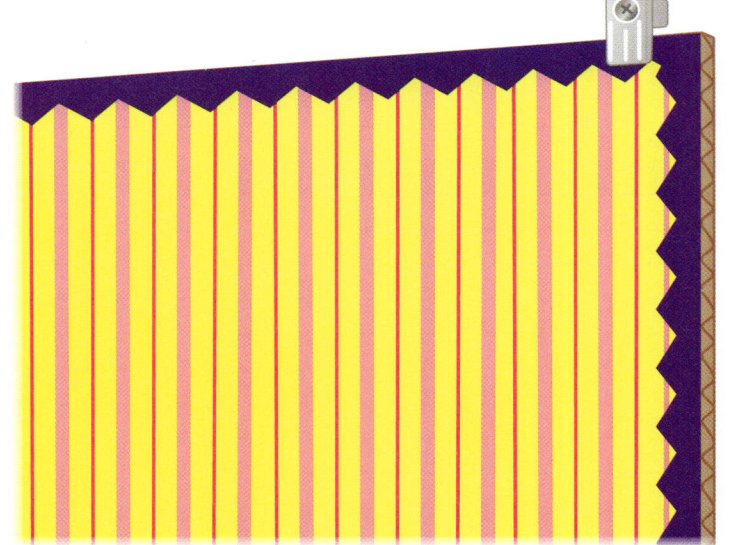

A Homemade Display
Display children's work with this lightweight, easy-to-make bulletin board. Cover a cardboard display board with paper or other material and then add a border. Simply hang the board on a wall using plastic mirror hangers!

Reusable Backgrounds
Looking for an inexpensive way to cover your bulletin boards? Use plastic tablecloths! This simple idea allows you to be creative with colors for any holiday or season. Best of all, when it's time to change the background, the tablecloth can be folded and stored for use at a later time!

It's a Material Thing!
Keep your bulletin boards looking like new all year long with fabric! Available in a wide range of colors and patterns, most fabrics are durable, reusable, and washable too. Find fabric with a pattern that is perfect for a holiday or theme and attach a permanent heading to it. After you take down the display, store the fabric until next year!

Letters File
Storing bulletin board letters is a snap with this handy tip: Store them in a file or recipe box with alphabetical dividers. Place the letters in their corresponding sections to keep them organized so they are easy to find when you need them!

Border Tubs
Plastic containers from ready-to-use frosting are ideal for storing bulletin board borders. Simply roll up the border and tuck it inside a container; then tape a piece of the border to the outside of the container. You can see at a glance what borders you have!

Welcome to School

Provide each child with a white crayon cutout (patterns on page 74) and have her color her crayon her favorite color. Personalize each youngster's crayon. Then post a large crayon box cutout and the colored crayons on your classroom door.

Personalize a hot-air balloon cutout (pattern on page 75) for each student and invite her to decorate it as desired. Then attach a photo of each child to the basket of the corresponding balloon. Before posting the balloons on a board, share with youngsters some things they will do this school year. Write several of the named activities on a cloud cutout and add it to the board.

In advance, collect a class supply of discarded compact discs (or make a class supply of compact disc cutouts). Using a permanent marker, personalize a compact disc for each child. Then attach the compact discs to a board using pushpins. Add a border of student-colored musical notes (patterns on page 75). If desired, invite each youngster to share his favorite song as you hang his compact disc.

Meet the Bunch!

Showcase your new bunch of preschoolers with this sweet display! Invite each youngster to fingerpaint a white construction paper circle purple by mixing red and blue fingerpaints. After the paint dries, personalize each student's circle. Display the circles so they resemble a bunch of grapes. Then add a stem cutout and leaf cutouts to complete the display.

Variations

- **A Bunch of Great Work!**
  Mount a sample of each student's work on a sheet of purple construction paper. Post the work samples around the grapes.

- **You've Been a Great Bunch!**
  For a year-end activity, have each youngster draw on a light purple circle cutout a picture of his favorite preschool memory. Display the completed circles so they resemble a bunch of grapes.

This preschool puzzle shows youngsters how they all fit together. Cut out and personalize a construction paper puzzle piece for each child, making sure that all pieces connect. (If desired, use the pieces of a large floor puzzle as patterns.) Have each youngster use tempera paint to make a handprint on his puzzle piece. After the paint dries, invite little ones to work together to assemble the puzzle. Use clear packing tape to secure the pieces, and post the completed puzzle.

What better way to showcase the students in your class than with a school of fish! Have each child use craft supplies to decorate a colorful fish cutout (patterns on page 76). After she adds desired details, write her name on her fish. Post the completed projects with a blue background.

Circle of Friends

Invite youngsters to be a part of your class's circle of friends. Have each student use a variety of art materials to decorate a child cutout (pattern on page 77) so it resembles himself. Post the completed projects in a circle formation. Point to a project on the display and invite youngsters to say something nice about the chosen friend.

✓ Student Activities

- **Counting:** Lead little ones in counting the cutouts to determine the number of students in the class. Then lead youngsters in counting the number of girls and the number of boys in the class. If desired, encourage students to compare the number of girls in the class to the number of boys.

- **Assessment of fine-motor skills:** After taking down the display, file the student-made cutouts. At the end of the school year, invite each youngster to decorate another cutout so it resembles herself. Compare the new cutouts to the ones made at the beginning of the school year to assess development of fine-motor skills.

Post a squirrel cutout on a board (enlarge the pattern on page 78). After each child makes an acorn (see below), write his name on it. Display the completed acorns around the squirrel.

Awesome Acorn

Supplies:
light brown acorn cutout (pattern on page 79)
brown tissue paper squares
diluted glue
paintbrush

Steps:
1. Lay a tissue paper square on the acorn.
2. Brush diluted glue over the tissue paper square.
3. Continue adding tissue paper squares to the acorn in this manner until the bottom of the acorn is covered.

BUSY LITTLE Bees

Parents and classroom visitors are sure to appreciate this honey of a schedule display! Make a hive cutout (pattern on page 80) for each activity your students routinely participate in. Label each hive with a separate activity and the time at which it occurs. Draw hands on each clock to correspond with the time. Then attach the hives to a wall. Invite each youngster to color a bee cutout (patterns on page 81). Personalize the bees and post them around the hives.

Who's the Helper of the Day?

This display is perfect for spotlighting a daily helper. Have each youngster sponge-paint a duck cutout (pattern on page 82). After the ducks are dry, help each youngster write her name on her duck and invite her to add desired details. Display the completed ducks on a pond cutout attached to the wall. Then attach a large feather to one of the duck's tails to indicate the helper of the day. Rotate the feather to a new duck each day to designate a different helper.

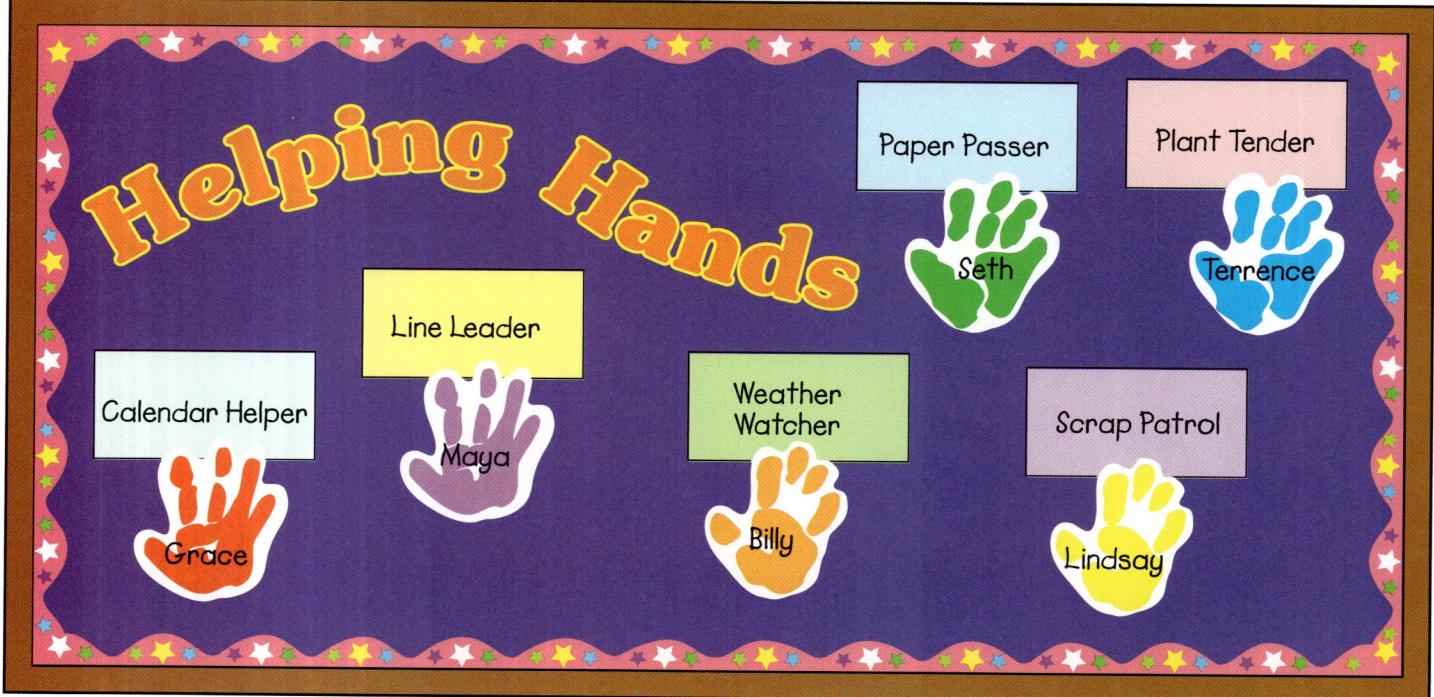

Invite each youngster to make a colorful handprint on a sheet of paper. After the handprints dry, personalize and trim each one. Laminate the handprints for durability if desired. Label a blank card for each classroom job you plan to assign and post the cards on a board. Attach a handprint below each card to indicate the student(s) assigned to each job. Store any extra handprints near the board. Assign new jobs as desired, using an established method of rotation.

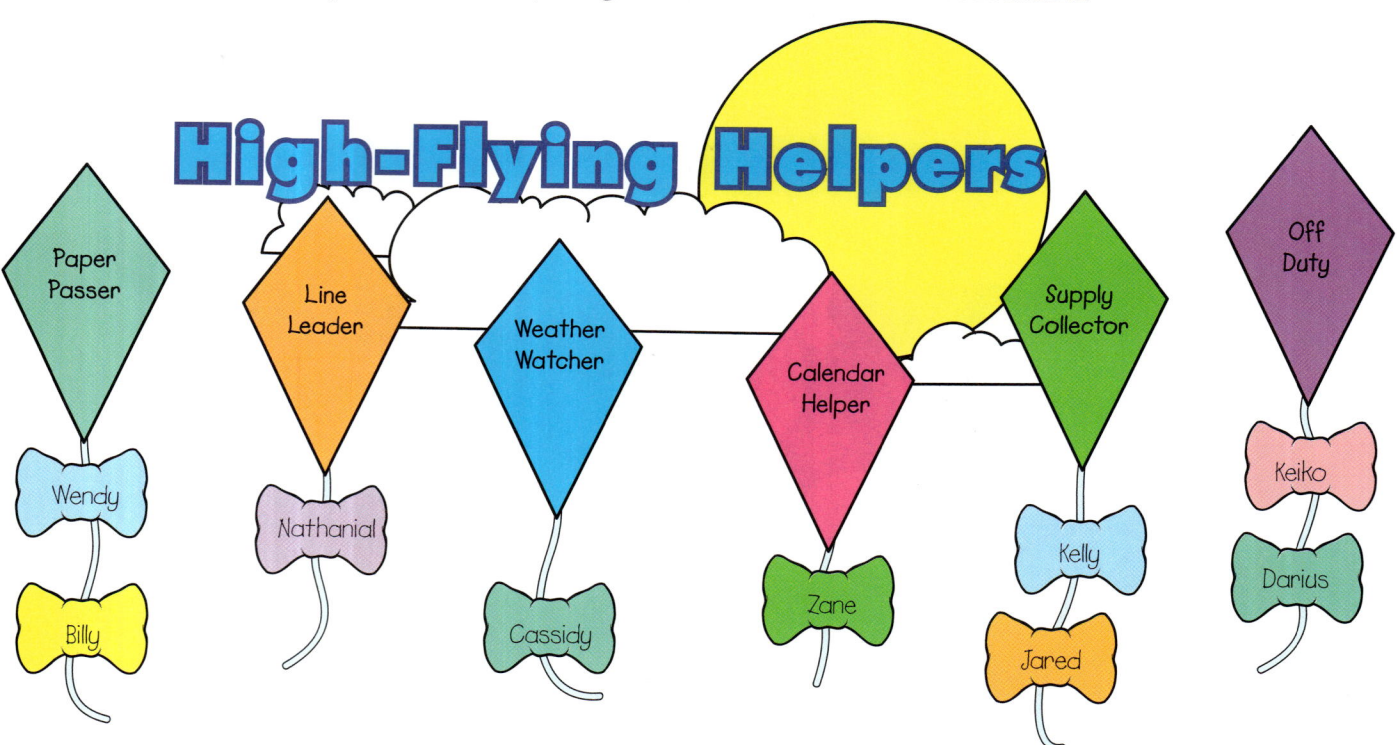

Prepare a kite cutout for each classroom job you plan to assign plus one extra. Label one kite "Off Duty" and each remaining kite with a desired job description. Add a yarn tail to each kite and display the kites on a wall. Then personalize a class supply of bow cutouts (patterns on page 83). Assign jobs by attaching the desired bows to the appropriate kites' tails; attach the remaining bows to the tail of the kite labeled "Off Duty." Change job assignments as desired.

Birthday Stars

Encourage little ones to feel like shining stars on their birthdays. Label a class supply of star cutouts (pattern on page 83) each with a different child's name and birthdate. Invite each youngster to use art supplies to decorate her star. Then cover a large tagboard star with foil. Display the large star on a wall and use Sticky-Tac to attach the smaller stars around it. On or before each child's birthday, help her move her star to the large star.

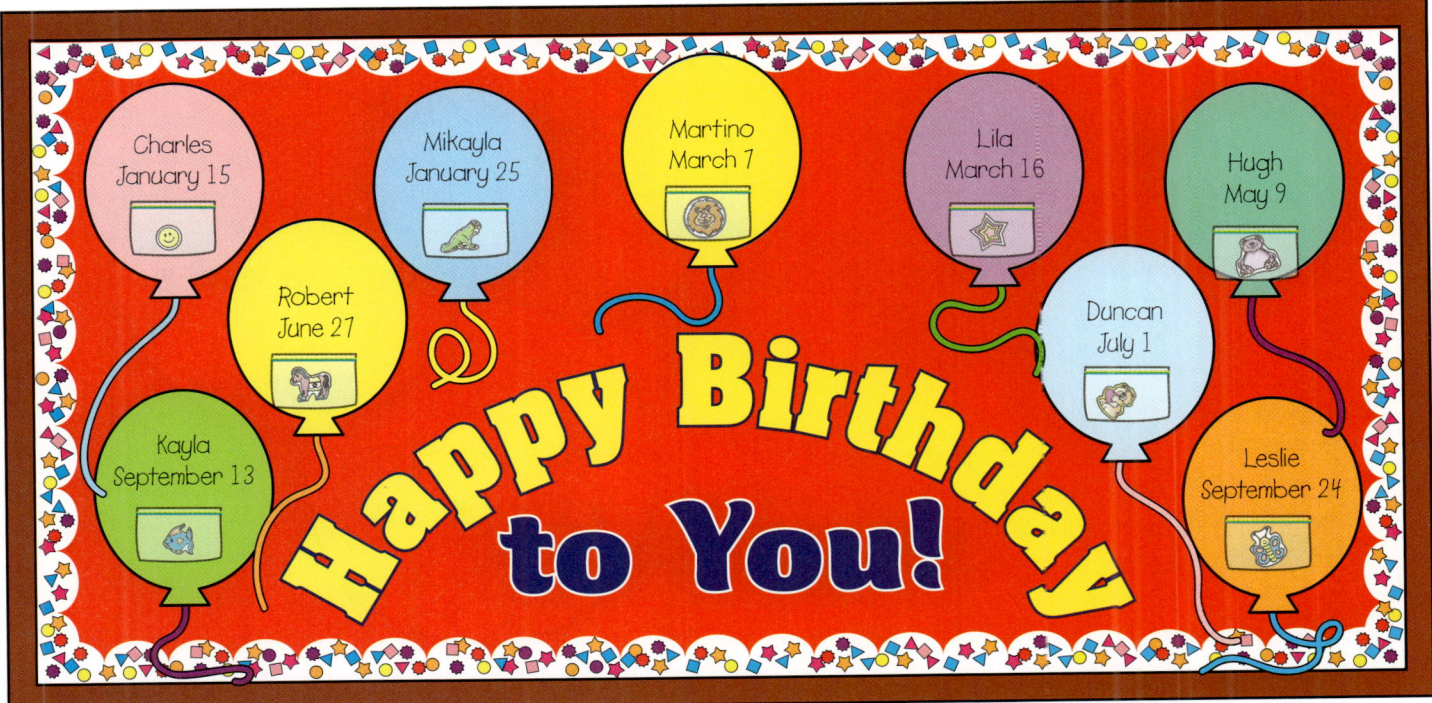

Acknowledge youngsters' birthdays and give them a special birthday treat. Write each child's name and birthdate on a separate balloon cutout. Attach the balloons to a board along with lengths of yarn. Staple a snack-size resealable plastic bag to each balloon. Slip a treat, such as a sticker, into each bag before sealing it. On or before each child's special day, take down his treat bag and present it to him.

Jot down a list of items you would like to have for use in your classroom. Post an enlarged wishing well cutout (pattern on page 84). Then label a supply of coin cutouts with different desired items. Post the coins around the wishing well. Invite parents and other visitors who would like to donate supplies for use in your classroom to choose a coin from the display, obtain the item, and bring it to you.

✳ Variations

- **More Classroom Wishes**
  On each of several coin cutouts, write a different classroom task that you would like parents to help with. Post the coins around the well.

- **Party-Time Wishes**
  Prior to a classroom party, write desired supplies on separate coin cutouts. Post the coins around the well. Encourage each parent to take a coin and return the item the day before the party.

For more year-round displays, be sure to check out the "Anytime" section beginning on page 61!

Fall

Invite youngsters to wiggle on in to your classroom! Personalize an apple cutout (pattern on page 85) for each child and cut a slit in each. Have each child color a worm cutout (pattern on page 85) and then help her thread the worm through the slit in her apple. Post the completed apples on your classroom door.

With a few simple changes and the variations below, this tree can be displayed all year! Post a bare tree cutout and add green leaf cutouts (patterns on page 86). Snap a photo of each youngster with his parent or guardian. Trim the photos and glue each one to a separate apple cutout (pattern on page 85). Invite each student to share his photo with the class. Then help him attach his apple to the tree.

✱ Variations

- **Falling for Great Books**
  Invite youngsters to use fall colors to sponge-paint a supply of leaf cutouts. Place the leaves near the board. After you read a book aloud, write the book's title on a leaf and post it on the tree.

- **Winter Wonderland**
  Invite each child, in turn, to share her favorite winter activity as you record her response on a snowflake cutout (patterns on page 86). Post the programmed flakes around the bare tree cutout.

- **Spring Has Sprung**
  Add green leaf cutouts to the tree. Invite each child to make a blossom; then help him display it on the tree.

- **We've Been Busy Bees!**
  For a year-end display, label a bee cutout (patterns on page 81) with each child's name. Have each child dictate her favorite activity from the past school year as you write it on her cutout. Post the bees around the leafy tree.

Pumpkin, Pumpkin

Count on this nutty display to provide math practice! Post an enlarged copy of the squirrel pattern (page 78) along with a basket cutout. Invite each child to color and cut out a copy of the acorn pattern on page 79. Use Sticky-Tac to attach the acorns to the display. Post a number card on the basket; then invite youngsters to move the appropriate amount of acorns to the numbered basket. Change the number card as desired.

Use the squirrel cutout again. See pages 10 and 25.

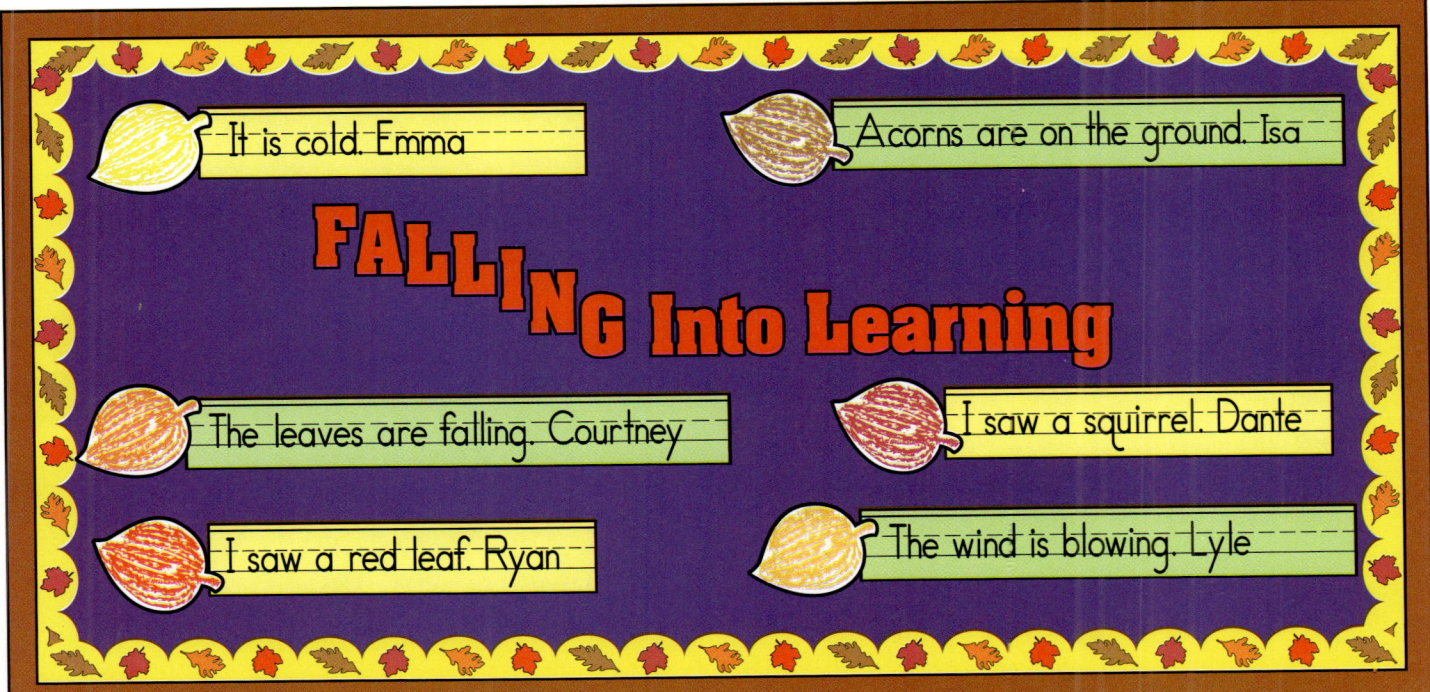

Focus on the seasonal changes autumn brings by taking little ones outside on a fall day. After returning to the classroom, invite each child to color a leaf cutout (patterns on page 86) to match a leaf he saw outside. Then have him share something he noticed outside as you record his response on a sentence strip. Write each child's name on his strip and display it near his leaf.

An adorable scarecrow and student-made crows are the focus of this autumn display. Post an enlarged copy of the scarecrow pattern from page 87 on a board with a white picket-fence cutout. Help each child make a crow (see below) and then post the crows on the board.

Cute Crow

Supplies:
two 9" x 12" sheets of black construction paper
3 orange triangles (beak and feet)
white chalk
scissors
glue

Steps:
1. Use the chalk to trace your foot on one sheet of black paper. Cut out the resulting crow body.
2. Use the chalk to trace your hands on the other sheet of black paper. Cut out the resulting wings.
3. Glue the wings, beak, and feet to the crow.
4. Use the chalk to draw eyes.

Share fire safety rules and list them on chart paper. Then have each child add black thumbprint spots to a dalmatian cutout (pattern on page 88). Invite her to color the dalmatian's hat and then help her add her name. Post the completed dalmatians around the chart for a fire safety reference.

Spin a splendid display by attaching a yarn web to a board. Then have each student make a spider by painting his hands (except for his thumbs) with black tempera paint, and pressing his hands with his thumbs overlapping on a sheet of white construction paper. After the paint is dry, trim around the spiders. Invite youngsters to add eye stickers or sticky-dot eyes. Attach the student-made spiders to the web.

This pumpkin patch helps youngsters recognize their classmates' names. Have each child paint a pumpkin cutout (pattern on page 89). After the paint dries, glue a trimmed photo of each child to her pumpkin and label the pumpkin with her name. Then string lengths of green yarn on a board to make vines. Attach the pumpkins and some leaf cutouts to the vines to complete the display.

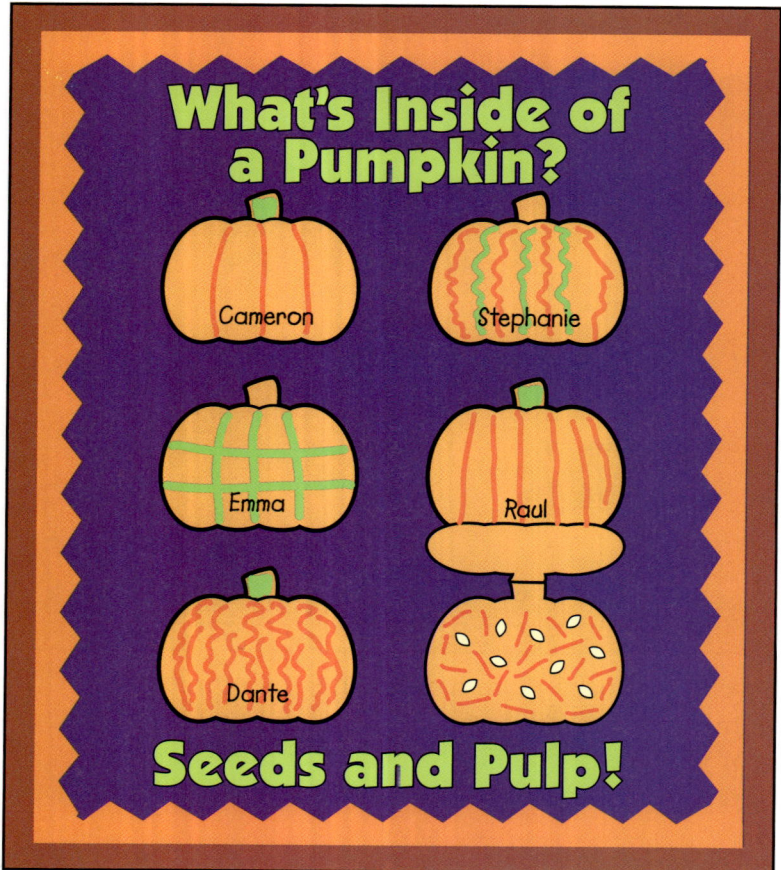

If your little ones explore the inside and outside of a pumpkin in your classroom, follow up with this display. Prepare two pumpkin cutouts for each child (pattern on page 89). Have each child glue short lengths of orange yarn (pulp) and a few pumpkin seed cutouts to one of the pumpkins. Ask him to add details to the other pumpkin so it resembles the outside of a pumpkin. Then help him staple the stems of the two pumpkins together. Display the completed pumpkins so they can be opened.

Your youngsters will adore this marvelous mummy! Make an extra large mummy cutout. (If desired, enlarge the child pattern on page 77.) Invite students to glue torn strips of white crepe paper to the cutout so it resembles a mummy. Cut two black eyes from construction paper and glue them to the mummy's face. Mount the completed mummy on your classroom door.

A Forest of Families

In advance, ask each child's parent or guardian to send a family photo to school. Have each youngster use fall colors to sponge-paint a tree cutout (pattern on page 90). After the paint dries, attach each child's family photo to his tree. Ask each child to share something he likes to do with his family and record his response on a copy of one of the recording sheets on page 91. Post each student's recording sheet on the trunk of his tree.

Invite youngsters to paint like the Native Americans did by making a buckskinlike painting. Help each child tear the corners off a 12" x 18" sheet of white construction paper and crumple the paper into a ball. Have her open the paper and use watercolors to paint a colorful sunset on the resulting buckskin. After each child's painting is dry, post it on a prepared board.

Stuffed With Thankfulness

We are thankful!
Sharon is thankful for her mom.
Lynn is thankful for her friends.
Kelly is thankful for her dog, Sadie.
Victor is thankful for his teachers.

Ask each youngster, in turn, to share something he is thankful for. Record students' responses on a large cornucopia cutout. Attach the cornucopia to a wall and add fruit cutouts. Help each child make a turkey (see below) and then post the turkeys around the cornucopia.

Stuffed Turkey

Supplies:
head, feet, and a supply of feather cutouts (patterns on page 92)
two 9" paper plates
newspaper
brown tempera paint
paintbrush

Steps:
1. Paint the bottom of the plates brown and set them aside to dry.
2. Color the head, feet, and feather cutouts. Glue the head and feet to one plate, as shown, and the feathers to the second plate.
3. Staple the two plates together, leaving a small opening.
4. Stuff crumpled newspaper into the opening until the desired effect is achieved.
5. Staple the opening between the two plates.

To prepare for this math-themed bulletin board, use the feather pattern on page 92 to make a supply of feather cutouts. Use the pattern on page 93 to make a turkey cutout for each child. Ask each youngster to choose a desired number of feathers between one and five and glue them to her turkey. Then help her count the feathers and label her turkey with the corresponding numeral. Post the completed turkeys on a board.

If Turkeys Could Talk, Here's What They'd Say!

Invite youngsters to imagine what a turkey might say if he could talk. Have each child make a turkey by painting his palm and thumb brown and his fingers a variety of colors (feathers). Then have him make a handprint on a sheet of bulletin board paper. After the paint is dry, have each child use markers to add details to his print so it resembles a turkey. Draw a speech bubble near each turkey's mouth. Ask each child what his turkey might say and write his response in his turkey's speech bubble. If desired, draw a fence around the turkeys to complete the display. Trim the paper and post it on a wall.

Winter

Welcome winter with a wonderful display of winter wear! Cut out a class supply of colorful construction paper clothing patterns (page 94). Invite each child to choose one of each type of clothing. Then have her glue her clothing to a 12" x 18" sheet of construction paper and draw a head and legs. Display the projects on a board along with an enlarged copy of the squirrel pattern on page 78. If desired, add some winter wear to the squirrel.

Use the squirrel cutout again. See pages 10 and 17.

For this sweet door display, attach brown packaging paper on and above your classroom door so it resembles a gingerbread house. Mount white bulletin board border to the top of the house to make frosting details. Then have youngsters use art materials to decorate candy cutouts (patterns on page 95). Mount these sweet crafts to the door. Add student-made gumdrop cutouts around the door to complete the gingerbread house.

To make this Hanukkah-themed display, have each youngster press her hand in blue paint and make a print on white construction paper; then have her make an extra thumbprint next to the handprint as shown. When the paint is dry, cut around the print and then use a black permanent marker to label each print with one of the Hebrew letters traditionally found on a dreidel. Then have each youngster decorate the print with silver glitter and tape a length of curled ribbon to the resulting dreidel's point. Mount the dreidels on a wall for a festive display.

This winter's night is awash in color with this lovely display of lights! Have each youngster make draping lines of glue on a black construction paper house cutout. Next, encourage her to sprinkle colorful hole-punch dots and gold glitter on the glue. Instruct her to shake off the excess dots and glitter. When the glue is dry, attach the houses to a bulletin board showing a snowy night scene. If desired, add a border of colorful lights.

To make this giggle-inducing bulletin board, take a close-up photo of each youngster's head. Enlarge and then trim the photos. Next, have each student press her hands in brown paint and make handprints on construction paper. When the paint is dry, cut out the prints and have each youngster glue them to either side of his photograph so they resemble antlers. Display the resulting projects on a board with a night sky.

Classroom visitors will run, run, run as fast they can to see this adorable display! Invite each youngster to use craft materials to decorate a gingerbread cookie cutout (patterns on page 96). Display the completed cookies on a wall so they look as if they are running on a path. To promote oral language, invite each child, in turn, to describe his cookie to classmates. Then ask a student to pretend to run to the display and "catch" the corresponding cookie.

Our Christmas Tree!

It takes teamwork to make this "tree-mendous" holiday display! Attach a supersize evergreen tree cutout to your wall. Provide access to construction paper scraps and strips, tape, and other craft materials. Encourage youngsters to use the supplies to make paper chains and ornament cutouts; then help students attach the decorations to the tree. After each child makes a present (see below), add it to the display as well.

Pleasing Presents

Supplies:
self-stick gift bow
construction paper square
2 construction paper strips
curling ribbon
shallow pan of paint
glue

Setup:
Knot several lengths of curling ribbon together to make a brush.

Steps:
1. Dangle the ends of the curling-ribbon brush in the paint.
2. Drag or gently bounce the brush across the construction paper square. Repeat until a desired effect is achieved.
3. Glue the strips to the square so they resemble ribbon.
4. Attach the gift bow.

Not only is this display fun to look at, but it also provides youngsters with math practice! Have each child use watercolors to paint a gumdrop cutout. After the paint is dry, invite her to brush diluted glue over the gumdrop and sprinkle it with clear glitter. Display the finished gumdrops in a mountain formation with the title shown. Encourage children to visit the display and count the gumdrops. Periodically remove or add gumdrops for extra counting practice.

Student Activities

- **Counting by color:** Ask students to name all of the colors in the gumdrop mountain. Then invite little ones to count how many gumdrops there are of each color. Record their responses and help them determine of which color there are the most or fewest.

- **Creative writing:** Encourage students to imagine they walked up to a mountain made of gumdrops. Have each child draw a picture of what she would do. Write her dictated response on her paper.

A Kwanzaa Celebration!

To make this Kwanzaa-themed display, give each youngster a square of brown construction paper and access to small squares of green, black, and red construction paper. Encourage each child to glue the small squares to the larger square. Next, have each child color and cut out a copy of one of the corn patterns on page 97. Display the finished mosaics together to make a large *mkeka,* a traditional Kwanzaa mat. To complete the display, attach the corn, or *muhindi,* to the mat.

No doubt this engaging board will prompt a flurry of smiling faces! Read aloud the classic story *The Polar Express* by Chris Van Allsburg. Then have each child color and cut out a copy of the boxcar pattern on page 99. Glue the boxcars and a train engine cutout (pattern on page 98) to a strip of black bulletin board paper. Place the prepared paper on a tabletop along with a shallow pan of white paint. Encourage youngsters to make white fingerprints (snowflakes) around the train. When the paint is dry, attach the display to a wall along with a white paper ground.

No doubt little ones will feel warm and cozy when they gaze at this adorable display! Enlarge the patterns on page 100 and then make two copies of the sock or mitten for each youngster. Attach a variety of textured materials to a tabletop and provide access to several unwrapped crayons. Help each youngster make rubbings of the materials on his socks or mittens to give them a textured appearance. After he cuts out his items, use clothespins to display them on a board decorated with a clothesline.

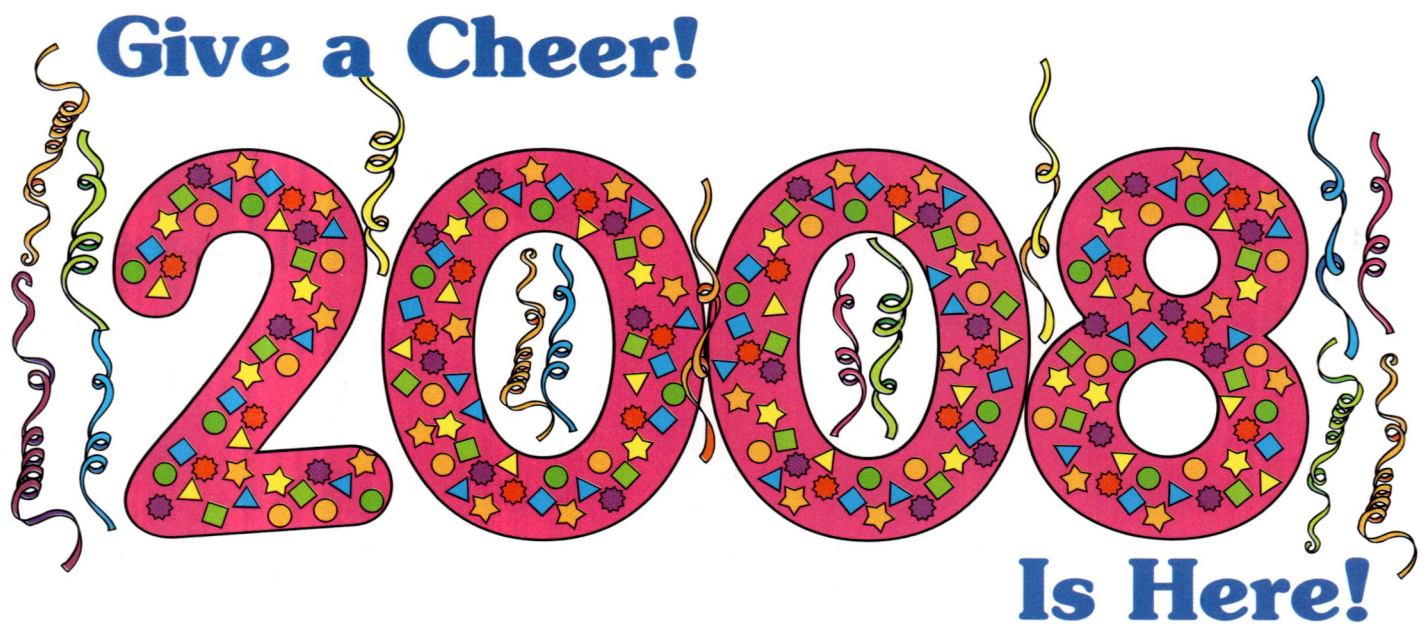

Here's a nifty way to commemorate the new year! Make large poster board number cutouts to show the new year and place the cutouts on a tabletop. Have youngsters cut scraps of construction paper and aluminum foil to make confetti. Place the confetti at the table along with several gluesticks. Encourage youngsters to glue confetti to the numbers. Mount the numbers on a wall and then add the title shown and embellishments.

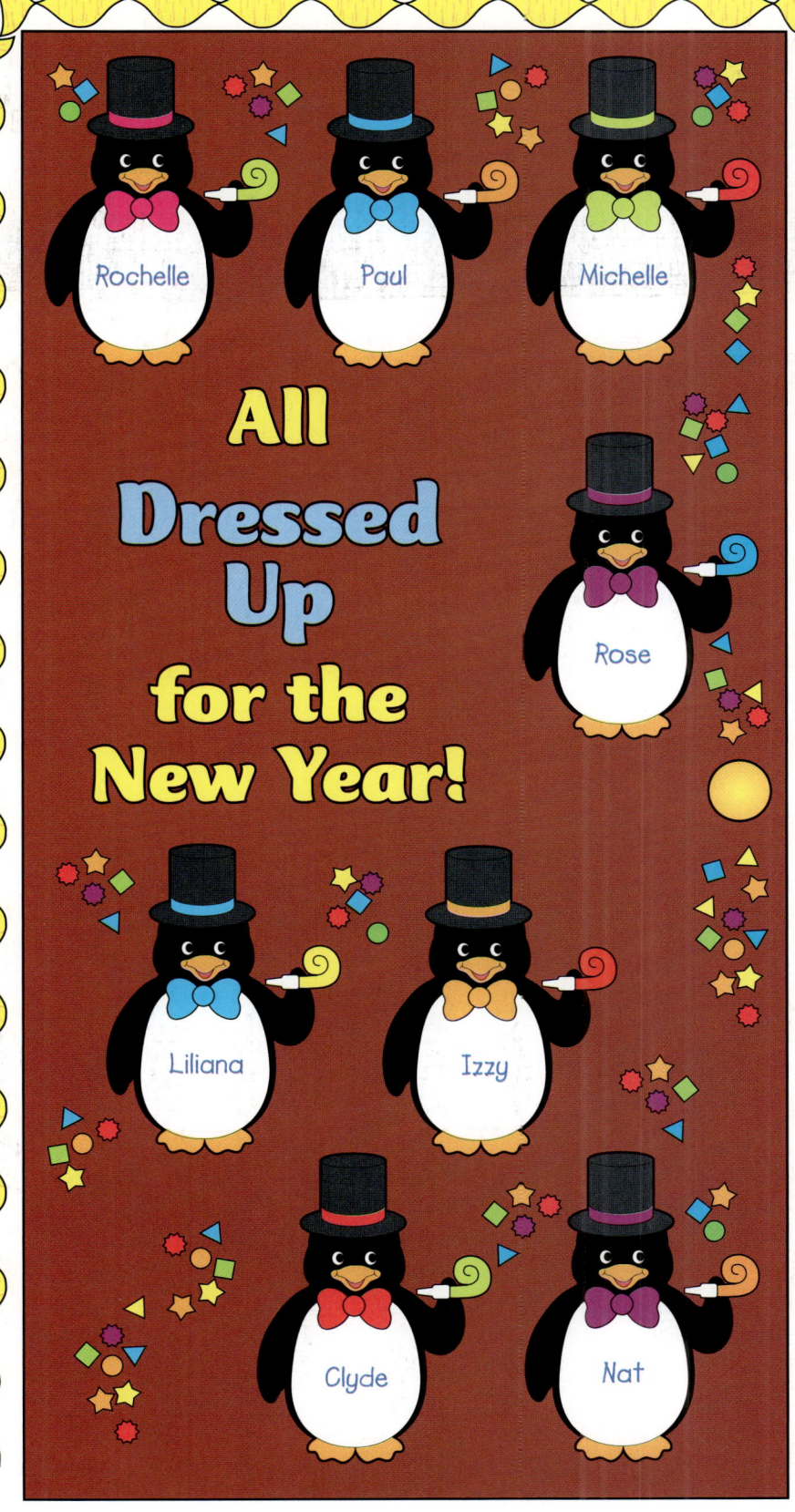

These cute little penguins are all dressed up for a New Year's party! For each child, cut out a construction paper copy of the penguin pattern on page 101 and one of the hat patterns on page 102. Have her decorate her penguin and hat. Next, help her glue the hat to the penguin and then tape a party blower to its flipper. Label each penguin with the corresponding child's name. Attach the crafts to your classroom door along with streamers and large scraps of construction paper (confetti).

The tracks this polar bear leaves behind are full of rhyming pairs! Brainstorm a list of rhyming word pairs with students. Then give each child two paw-print cutouts (patterns on page 104). Have him draw each picture from a rhyming pair on a separate print. Display each pair of prints along with an enlarged copy of the polar bear pattern from page 103.

✳ Variations

- **Bear Tracks**
  Give each child an enlarged copy of one of the paw-print patterns to cut out. Encourage him to glue crumpled tissue paper squares to his print. Then mount the prints and the polar bear on a board.

- **Follow the Bear Tracks**
  Have each child remove his shoes and step into a large pair of boots. Help him press the bottom of the boots in a shallow pan of paint. Then assist him as he walks across a length of bulletin board paper. When all youngsters have had an opportunity to add prints to the paper, attach it next to the bear-track display.

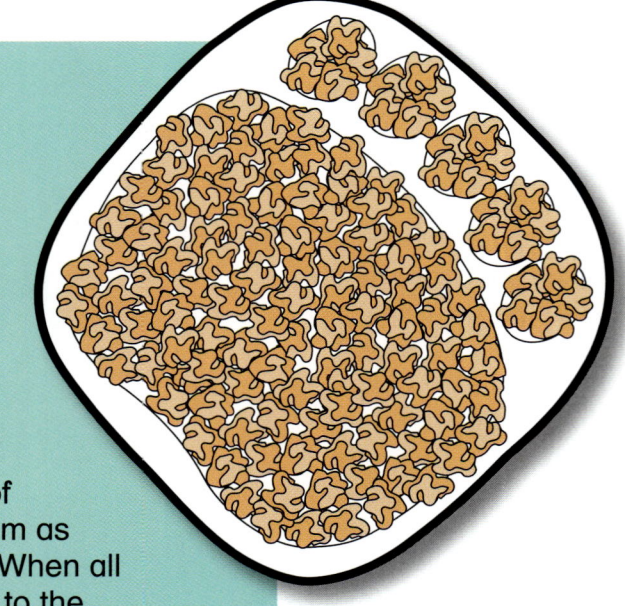

Have each youngster glue together two three-inch circles and one two-inch circle to make a snowpal. Then invite him to decorate his snowpal. (If desired, have each child attach a copy of one of the hat patterns on page 102 to his snowpal.) Encourage him to glue a pair of ice skate cutouts (page 102) to his snowpal. Then attach the finished snowpals to a board embellished with an aluminum foil pond.

Share the message of Martin Luther King Jr. with this heartfelt display. Have each youngster press her hands in paint colored similar to her skin tone. Then prompt her to make handprints on a heart cutout. Display the completed hearts on a wall to remind youngsters about this important person.

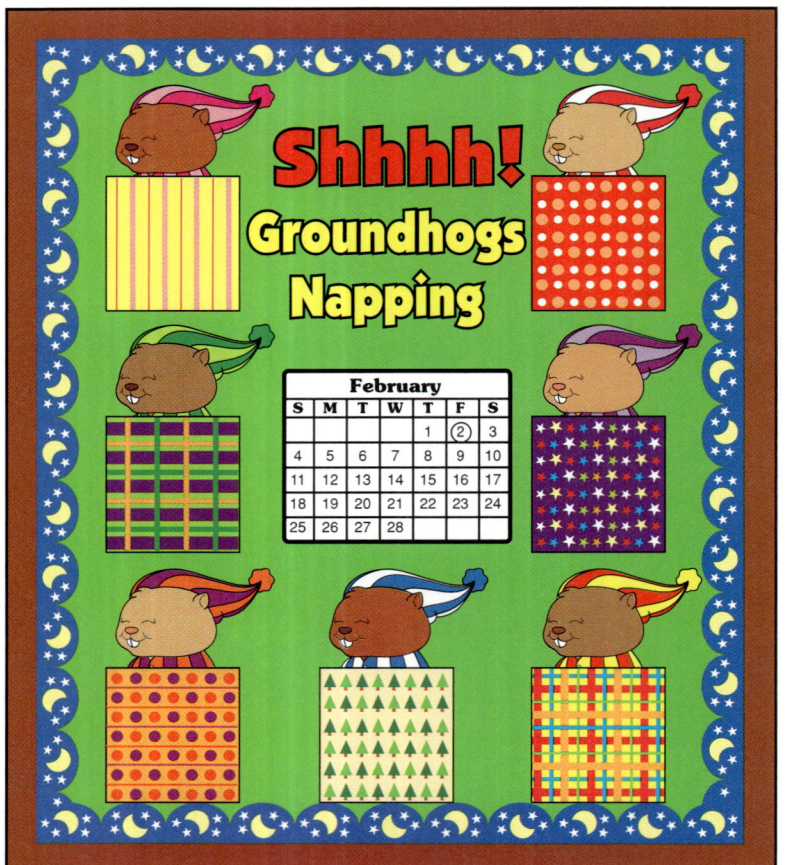

Put up this fun display well before Groundhog Day! For each child, cut out a copy of the groundhog pattern on page 105. After she colors her groundhog, instruct her to glue a piece of fabric (blanket) to the cutout. Display the finished groundhogs on a wall. Then circle Groundhog Day (February 2) on a calendar and add the calendar to the display. Now youngsters can see when the little critter will wake and give its yearly prediction.

For this dental health display, have students splatter-paint a length of colorful bulletin board paper using unused toothbrushes. When the paper is dry, attach it to a bulletin board. Take each youngster's photograph while he grins enthusiastically. Then trim each photo and glue it on a tooth cutout (pattern on page 106). Attach the teeth to the board. Next, have each student decorate several copies of the toothbrush pattern on page 106. To complete the display, use the toothbrushes to make a border.

Have a Sweet Valentine's Day!

This three-dimensional display is sure to be a favorite with your students! Mount a large heart cutout to a wall. Have each child make a chocolate candy craft (see below). Use tacks or double-sided tape to attach each three-dimensional craft to the heart so it resembles an oversize box full of chocolates.

Lovely Chocolate

Supplies:
foil cupcake holder
brown tissue paper
red pom-pom
glitter
white glue

Steps:
1. Drizzle a generous amount of glue in the bottom of the cupcake holder.
2. Crumple brown tissue paper into a ball and press it into the glue.
3. Drizzle glue on top of the tissue paper. Then sprinkle glitter on the glue.
4. Glue the pom-pom to the top of the craft.

This cute display tells the buzz about Valentine's Day! Instruct each child to paint black stripes and facial features on a yellow oval so the oval resembles a bee. Have each student add a paper stinger to his bee as well as pink heart-shaped construction paper wings. Ask each child to dictate a Valentine message as you write it on the wings. Mount the bees on a board for a heartfelt display.

No doubt Honest Abe would be proud to see this easy-to-prepare birthday board! Have each child use a variety of craft items to decorate a stovepipe hat cutout. When the glue is dry, mount the hats on a bulletin board.

Spring

Celebrate Dr. Seuss's birthday on March 2 with a read-aloud of *Green Eggs and Ham*. Then help each child cut out the patterns and recording sheet on page 107 and invite her to color the ham green. Next, have her glue a green circle to the egg and then glue the egg and the ham to a paper circle (plate). Mount the project and the recording sheet on a sheet of construction paper. Ask each child, "Would you like to eat green eggs and ham?" Then have her circle the appropriate symbol on the recording sheet. Display the completed projects on the board.

The Shamrock Showplace

Copy and cut out a green construction paper shamrock (pattern on page 108) for each student. Mix a small amount of green paint with glue. Invite each child to use the glue mixture to add to a shamrock an assortment of green art supplies, such as torn paper, crumpled tissue paper, dyed rice, pom-poms, yarn, felt, or foam shapes. Then post the shamrocks on a board along with an enlarged copy of the leprechaun pattern on page 109.

Preschool Leprechauns

To make a face of a leprechaun, paint the bottom of a child's hand green, the middle of his hand skin tone, and his fingers orange. Then have him press his hand down on a sheet of paper. When the paint is dry, cut around each handprint. Then have the child glue a photo of his face to the palm and draw details on the green paint to resemble a hat. Mount the resulting leprechauns on your classroom door to give everyone a cheerful St. Patrick's Day welcome!

Reinforce youngsters' understanding of positional words with this interactive display. Mount on a board a simple fence cutout and an enlarged copy of the barn pattern on page 111. After each child makes a lamb (see below), give her directions using positional words, such as place the lamb *beside* the fence or *between* the fence and the barn. Then have her use Sticky-Tac to attach her lamb to the display.

A Little Lamb

Supplies:
lamb patterns (page 110)
large white paper plate
cotton balls
glue
black crayon

Steps:
1. Draw a face on the head with the black crayon. Color the feet black.
2. Glue the head to the top of the plate.
3. Glue the feet to the bottom of the plate.
4. Glue cotton balls to the body and top of the head.

To prepare, tint several containers of water with various colors of food coloring. Invite each child to use eyedroppers to drip water in several colors on a light-colored construction paper kite. Then direct him to blow through a straw to move the drops around. When the kite is dry, help each child add a length of ribbon or crepe paper, and then mount each kite on a board to display the unique designs.

For this colorful display, draw a rainbow outline on a sheet of bulletin board paper. In turn, have each student remove his shoes and socks and step in a desired color of paint. Then assist him in walking across the corresponding color arch. After the paint is dry, cut around the rainbow. Then hang the completed project to display a masterpiece of fancy footwork!

Flowers need rain and sun. With this unique project, they get both! Display each child's rain-or-shine picture (see below); then simply lift the sheet filled with raindrops to add a little sunshine to your preschool flower garden!

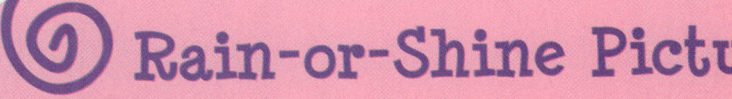 Rain-or-Shine Picture

Supplies:
wide-tooth comb
9" x 12" piece of waxed paper
9" x 12" piece of white construction paper
black and white paints mixed to make gray
assorted spring-colored paints
paintbrush
stapler

Steps:
1. Paint gray clouds at the top of the waxed paper.
2. Dip the teeth of the comb into the gray paint and drag it down the paper to create raindrops. Set the paper aside to dry.
3. Make a colorful handprint on the white paper. Paint a green stem and leaves under the handprint. Set the paper aside to dry.
4. Staple the waxed paper along the upper edge of the white paper.

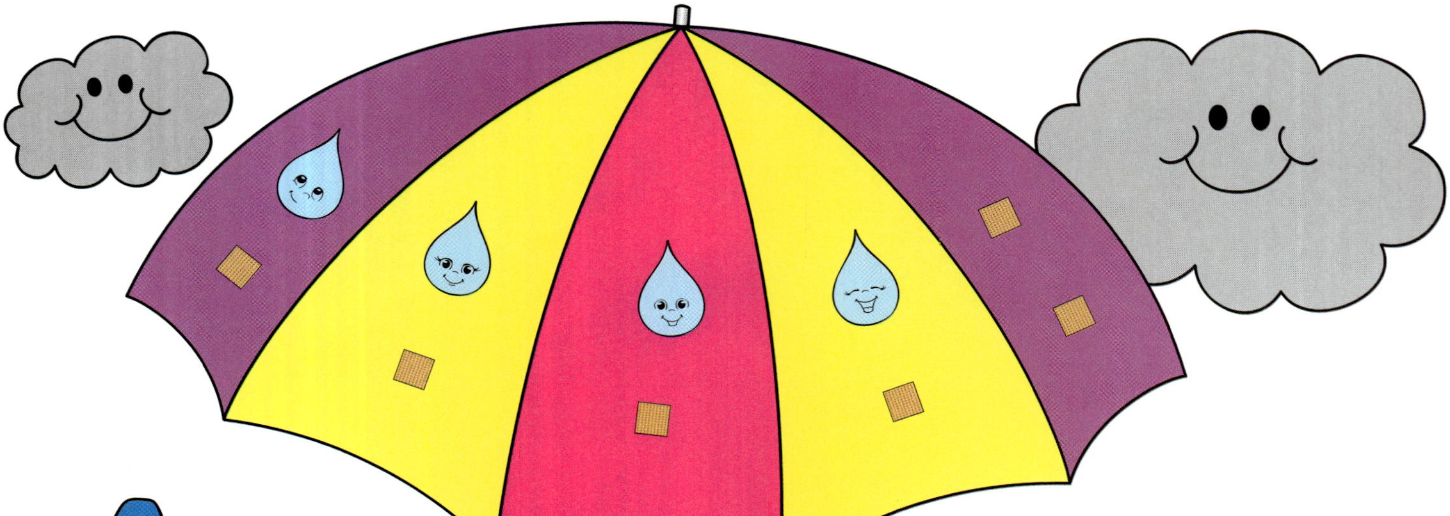

April Showers

Find out if it's a drizzle or a downpour when students count the raindrops on this math display! To prepare, make a large umbrella cutout and attach it to a wall. Cut out a supply of raindrops (patterns on page 112) from blue poster board. Attach the loop sides of Velcro fasteners to the raindrops and the hook sides of Velcro fasteners to the umbrella. To use the display, call out a number. Invite a child to count out that number of raindrops as she attaches them to the umbrella.

Inspire little ones' imaginations with this indoor mud mixture! Mix together a supply of brown paint and sand to make a mudlike paint. Invite youngsters to cut a puddle shape from brown construction paper and then to use the mixture to paint the cutout. Ask each child if she would like to play in the mud and why, and record her answers. Mount each child's mud puddle and response on a sheet of construction paper. Post the projects on a board along with an enlarged copy of the pig pattern on page 113.

Ten Lovely Ladybugs

Copy the ladybug patterns on page 114 on red tagboard. Write a different number from 1 to 10 on each body and draw a corresponding dot set on each pair of wings. Cut out the pieces and staple the matching wings to each body as shown. Mount the ladybugs in numerical order on a grassy display. To use the display, a child counts a dot set and then confirms the quantity counted by lifting the wings and checking the number.

✳ Variations

- **Ladybugs on the Move!**
  Add a tree, a rock, and a log (log pattern on page 115) to the display. Attach the loop side of Velcro fasteners to the ladybugs and the hook side of Velcro fasteners to various locations on the board. Then give directions using positional words—such as make the ladybug crawl *up* the tree, sit *on* the rock, or walk *across* the log—to direct students where to place their ladybugs on the display.

- **More or Fewer?**
  Place two ladybugs on the log. Invite a student to count the spots on each ladybug. Then lead youngsters to compare the number of spots to determine which ladybug has more spots and which ladybug has fewer spots.

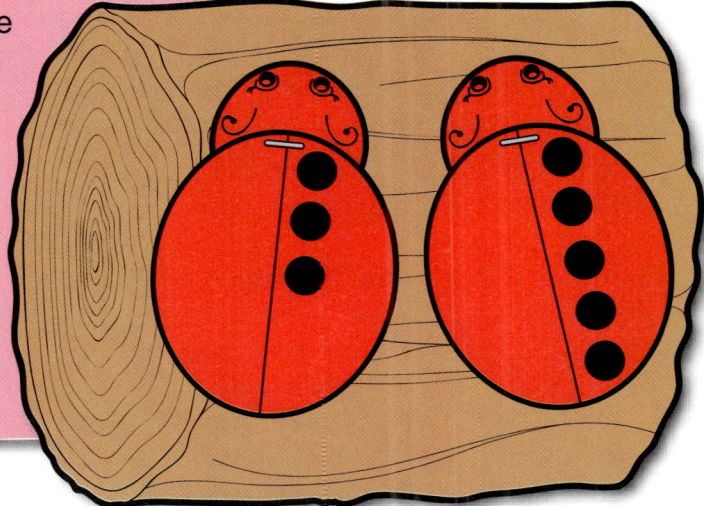

The ladybug with five spots has more!

Little ones create their very own preschool pond with this add-on board! Cut out one or more copies of the log pattern on page 115 to use with the display. For each child, copy the patterns on page 116 on white construction paper and the patterns on page 117 on green construction paper and cut them out. Over several days, invite students to make different pond animals (see below). Have students embellish each critter as desired. Add the projects to a board as they are completed.

Pond Critters

To make a fish, paint the fish cutout with watercolors and add details with a black marker.

To make a duck, glue yellow craft feathers to a duck cutout, and then glue on a paper beak and eye.

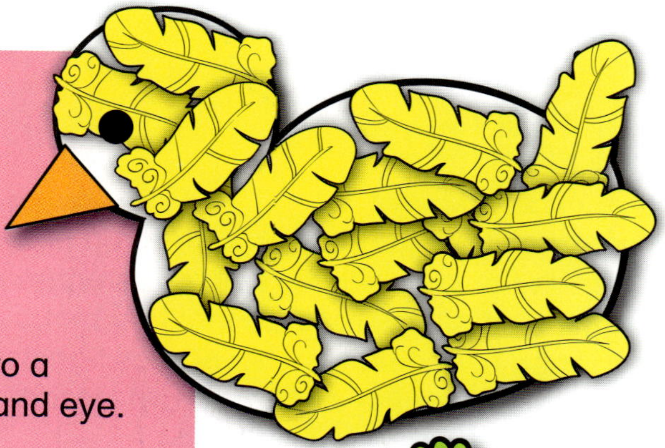

To make a turtle, attach the turtle patterns to a small paper plate. Paint the top of the plate with a mixture of green paint and glue, and then add tissue paper squares to the plate.

To make a frog, paint the frog cutout with a mixture of green paint and sand and then add spots with a black marker.

Just like a caterpillar, your preschoolers' hands and feet magically transform into beautiful butterflies! Help each child make a butterfly (see below). Then mount each butterfly on a wall for a delightful spring display.

Beautiful Butterflies

Supplies:
colorful construction paper
colorful tissue paper squares
6" length of colorful pipe cleaner
crayons
glue
tape

Setup:
Trace around each child's shoe on construction paper. Trace her hand four times on a different color paper. Cut out the tracings.

Steps:
1. Position the foot cutout (body) with the small end at the top for the head. Glue two hand cutouts (wings) to each side.
2. Use crayons to draw a face.
3. Fold a pipe cleaner (antenna) in half and tape it to the back of the head.
4. Crumple tissue paper squares and glue them to the wings.

"Bee" a Good Friend!

This simple display encourages friendship and unity among students. Draw a large beehive shape on a sheet of yellow bulletin board paper. In turn, have each student apply brown paint to a piece of bubble wrap and then press the bubble wrap on the bulletin board paper. After the paint is dry, cut around the beehive and attach it to a wall. Personalize a class supply of bee cutouts (patterns on page 81) and post them on the display. Each time a student exhibits a friendly "bee-havior," write what she did on a sticky note and attach the note to her bee.

Student Activities

- **Dictating to a prompt:** Invite each student to respond to a prompt, such as "I can be a good friend if I…" or "I was a good friend today when I…"

- **Vocabulary:** Encourage each child to help you create word cards by naming words that describe how to be a friend. To do the activity, choose a card and then invite two students to role-play the behavior named on the card.

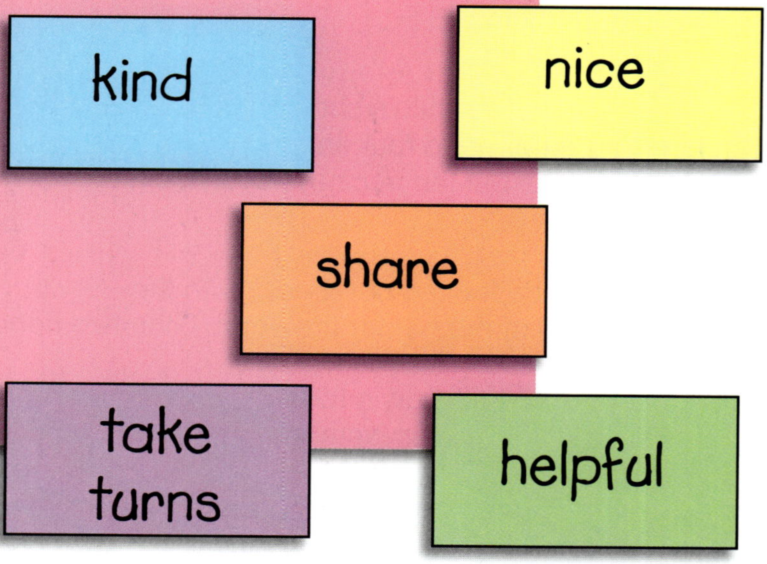

For each child, copy the bee pattern (page 118) on yellow construction paper and copy the wing patterns (page 118) on white construction paper. Invite each child to cut out the patterns. Then help him write his name on a wing. Attach the wings to the body and add pipe cleaner antennae. Encourage him to draw a face on his bee and to add black stripes to the body. Help him attach his bee to the top of a 9" x 12" sheet of black construction paper. Mount the projects and use them to display students' work.

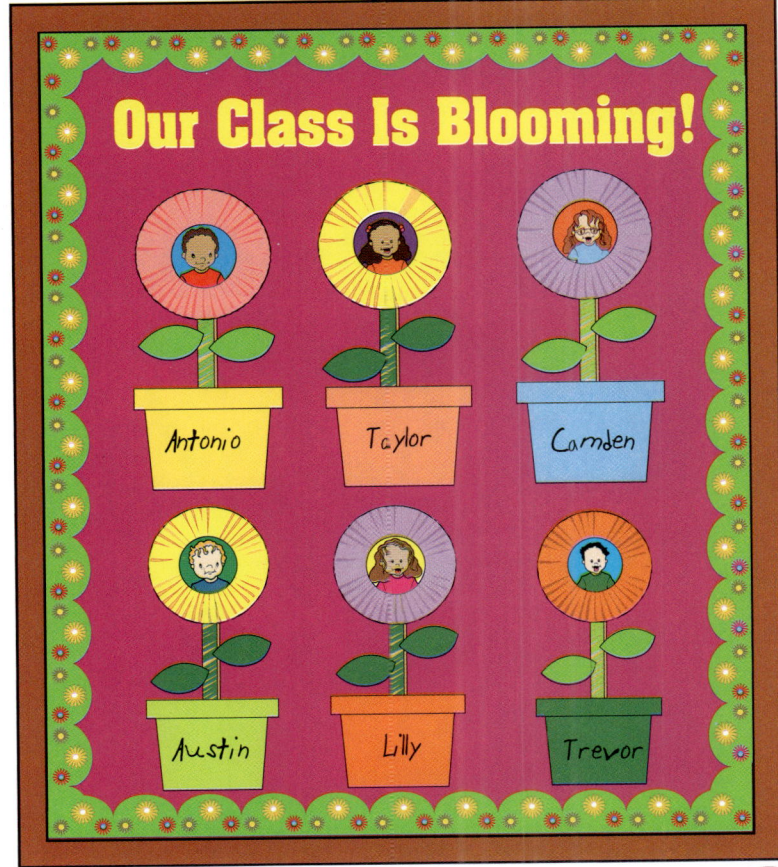

Showcase your preschoolers with a flower garden! Invite each child to color a craft stick green. Help her glue a flattened cupcake liner to one end of her craft stick and then glue a photo of her face to the center of the liner. After she glues construction paper leaves to the craft stick, help her attach the resulting flower to a flowerpot cutout. Mount the projects to create a classroom flower display.

FLOWER POWER!

To prepare, tint several containers of water with various colors of food coloring. Invite each child to fold a white coffee filter in half several times. Then assist her in cutting the filter to scallop the edge. Instruct her to dip one end of the folded filter in one color and the opposite end in another color. Have her unfold the coffee filter and set it aside to dry. To complete the flower, encourage each child to cut out paper leaves, tape the leaves to a straw, and tape the straw to the filter. Arrange the resulting flowers on a board to create a colorful array of blooms!

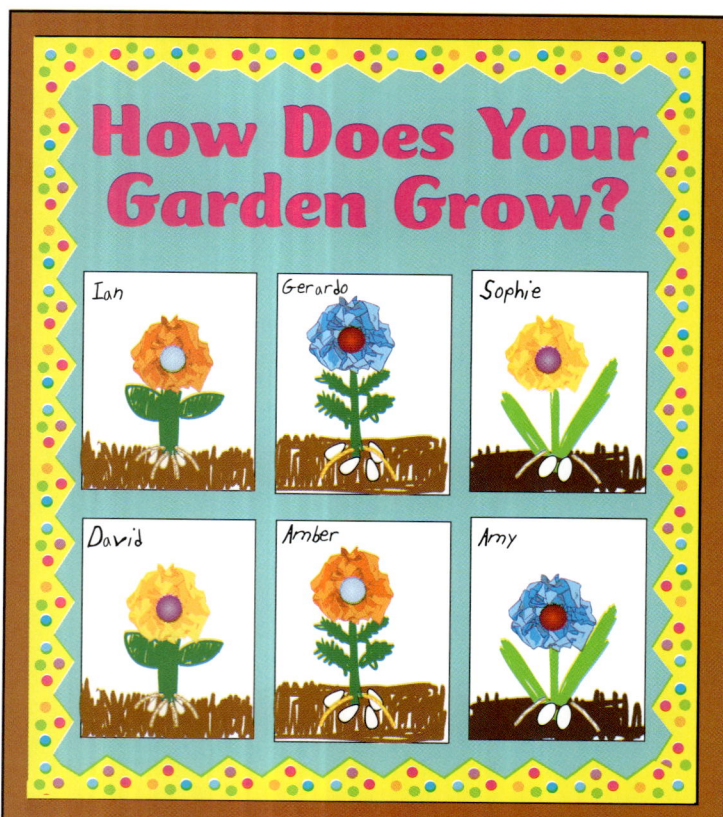

Preschoolers create flowers from the roots up! Have each child use a mixture of brown paint and sand (dirt) to paint along the bottom of a sheet of construction paper. Direct him to glue paper flower seeds to the dirt. Then have him glue small pieces of yarn (roots) to the seeds. Next, encourage him to paint a stem and leaves. To complete the project, instruct him to glue a colorful pom-pom to the top of the stem (bud) and then to glue crumpled tissue paper around the bud to show it has developed into a flower. Mount the projects on a board and refer to them to review how a flower grows.

End of the Year

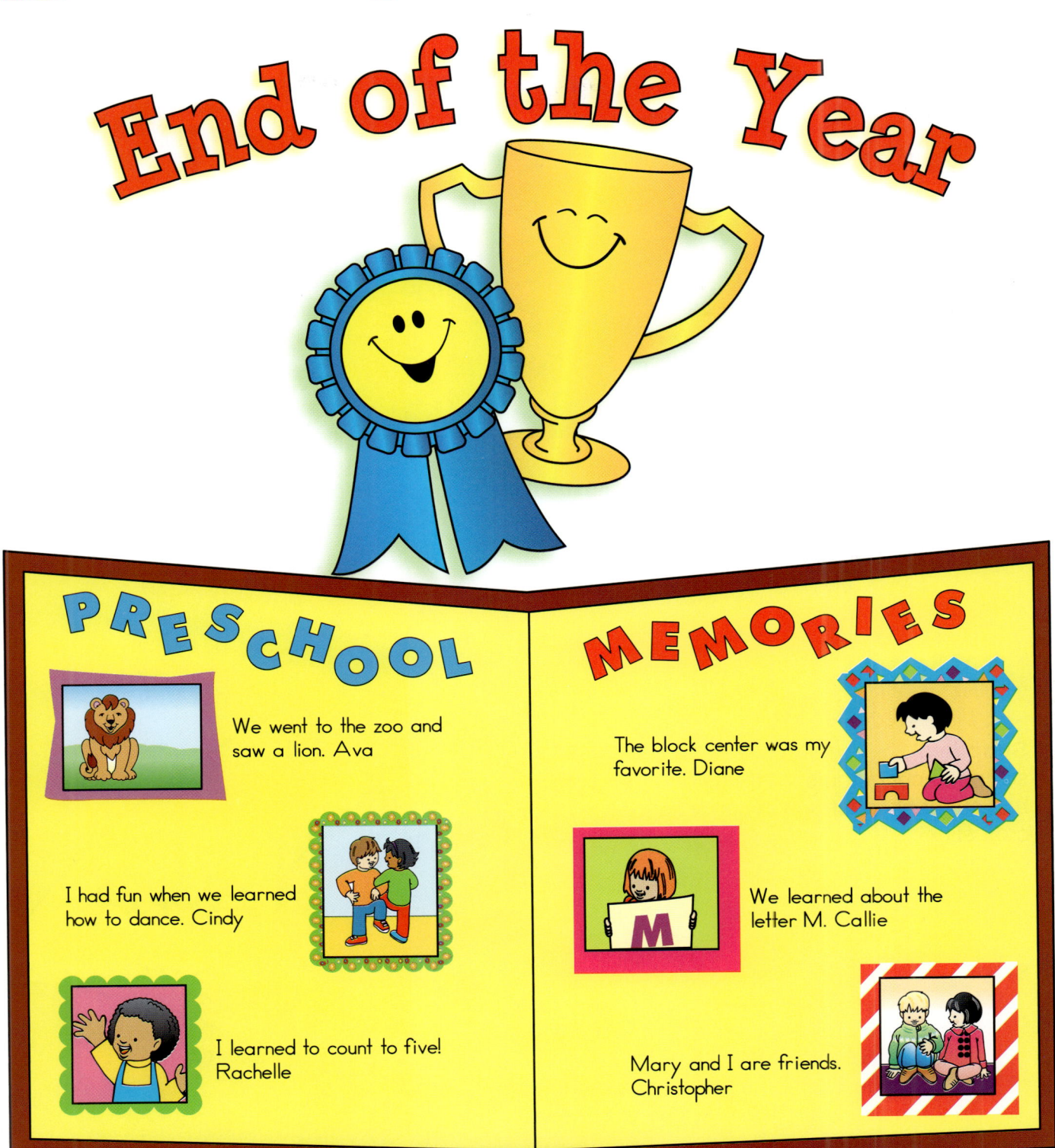

Display preschoolers' memories on an oversize scrapbook page. To make the page, fold a length of bulletin board paper in half and then unfold it to create a crease in the middle of the paper. Gather a supply of photos from the school year and invite each youngster to choose his favorite photo. Have him glue it to a piece of colorful scrapbook paper. Display youngsters' photos on the scrapbook page. To complete the display, write a child-dictated caption near each photo.

SAILING INTO SUMMER!

This seafaring display showcases youngsters' summer plans! To prepare, trim strips of bulletin board paper so they resemble waves and attach them to a wall. Help each child make a sailboat (see below). Personalize the sailboats and mount them on the waves.

Sailboat

Supplies:
sail and boat cutouts (patterns on page 119)
half sheet of construction paper
craft stick
crayons
scissors
glue

Steps:
1. Use crayons to draw a picture of something you plan to do this summer on the triangular sail cutout.
2. To make an additional sail, trace one hand on the half sheet of paper and cut out the tracing.
3. Glue the boat and sail cutouts to a craft stick.

52

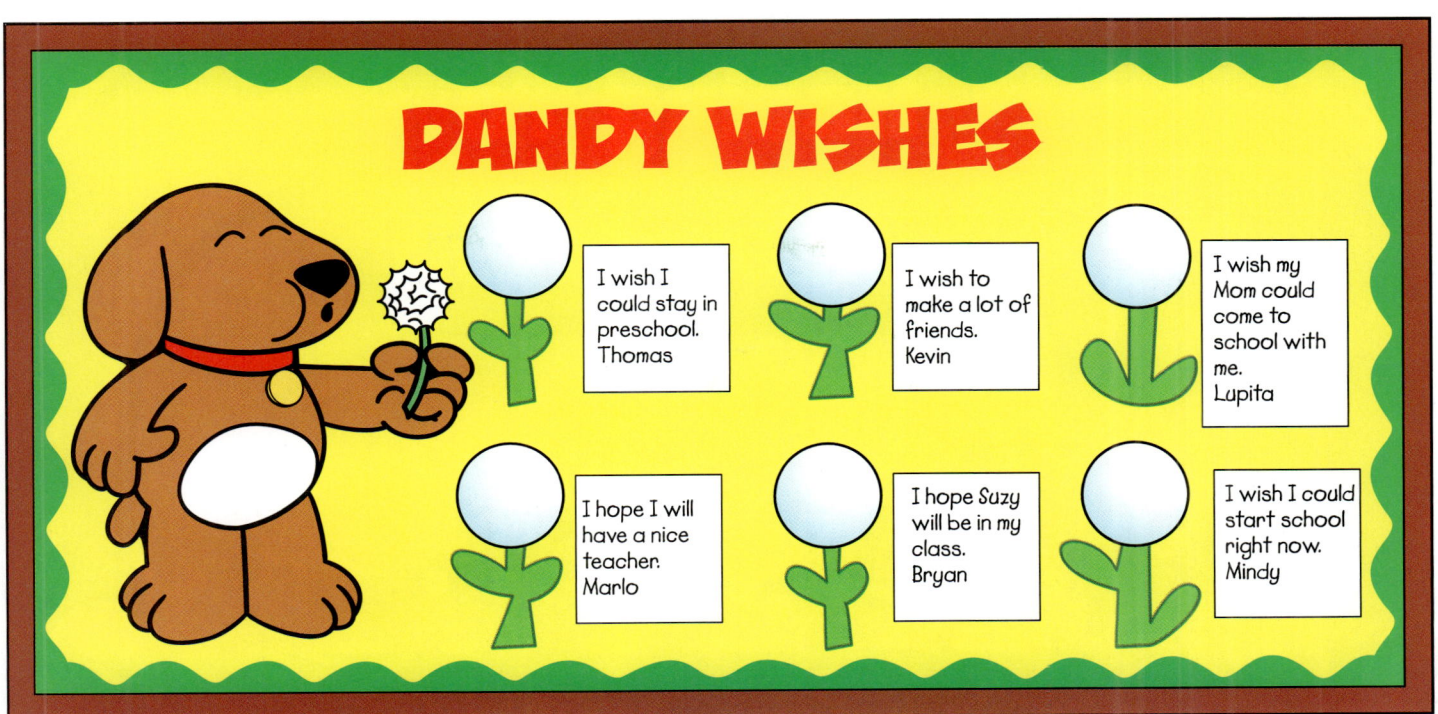

Little ones make wishes for the next school year with these three-dimensional dandelions. For every two students, cut a small foam ball in half to create two dandelion blooms. Have each youngster glue his bloom to construction paper and draw an outline of a stem and leaves. Trim around each child's dandelion and hot-glue it to a board decorated with an enlarged copy of the puppy pattern on page 120. Then ask each student to make a wish for the next school year. Write each child's response on a blank card and post it beside his dandelion.

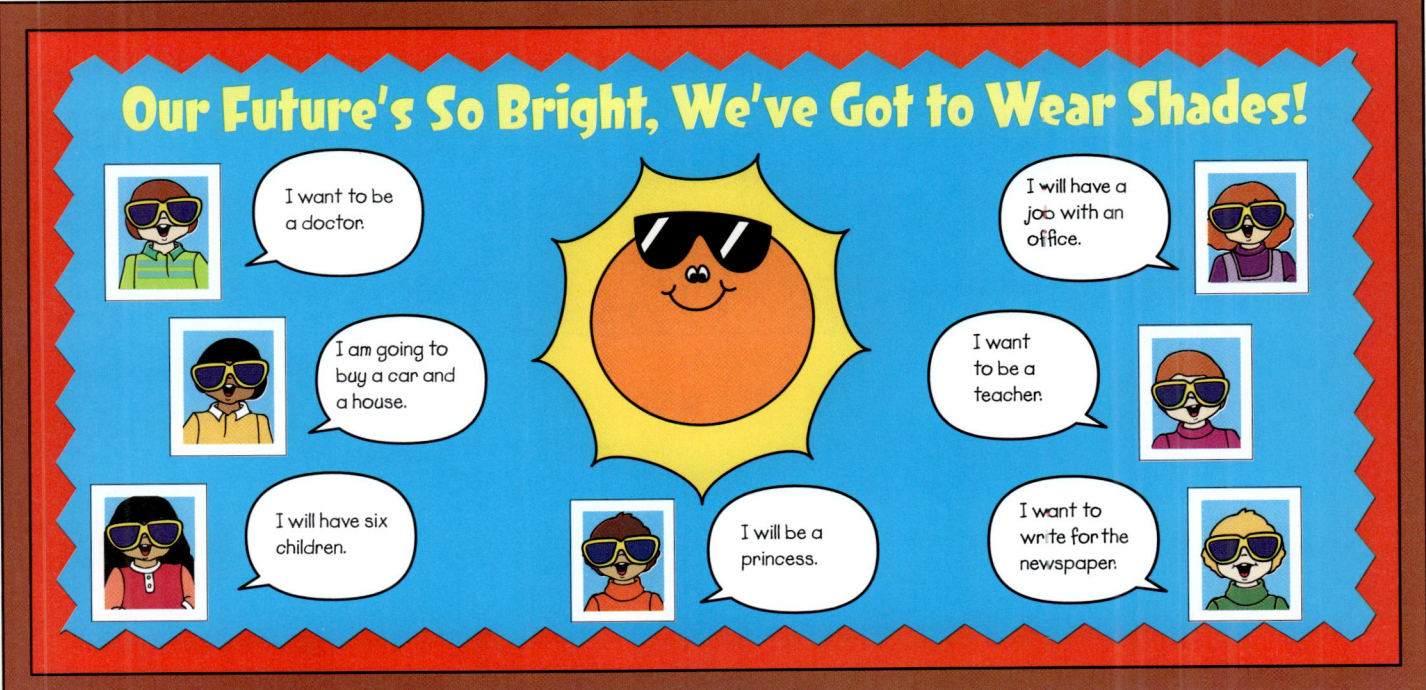

In advance, snap a photo of each child wearing a pair of oversize sunglasses. Mount the photos on a board around an enlarged copy of the sun pattern on page 121. Ask each child to describe what she thinks her life will be like when she grows up. Write her response on a speech bubble cutout. Post the speech bubbles alongside the corresponding photos.

Use the sun cutout again. See page 68.

Racing To Kindergarten

To make a racetrack, invite youngsters to help paint a piece of bulletin board paper black. After the paint dries, cut the paper into a large oval, cut out the middle, and paint white dashes around the resulting track. Have each student color a racecar cutout (patterns on page 122) with bright-colored crayons. Add each child's name and a desired number to his racecar. Mount the track on a wall and attach the cars to the track.

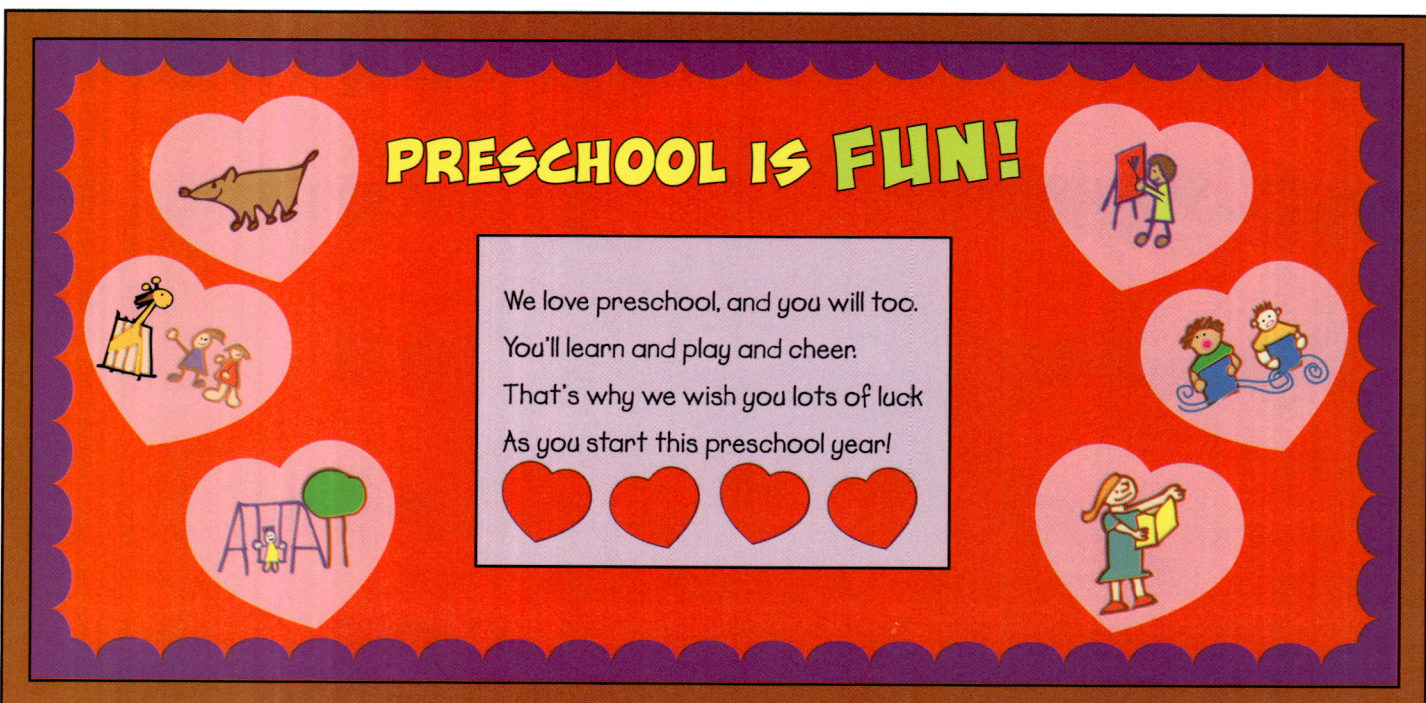

Display this bulletin board at the end of the school year; then leave it up to welcome your new class the following school year. Have each child draw a picture of what he liked best about preschool on a heart cutout. Then post the hearts around the poem shown.

Summer

Youngsters practice number recognition and counting with this interactive wall display. Post five numbered basket cutouts along with a bush cutout and a mouse character (enlarge the pattern on page 123). Then use the patterns on page 124 to make enough strawberry cutouts to match the numbers on the baskets. Use Sticky-Tac to attach the strawberries to the bush. To use the board, a youngster picks berries off the bush and attaches the appropriate number of strawberries to each basket.

Use the mouse cutout again. See page 66.

Your students will be proud to be part of this patch! Twist green crepe paper to make vines. Mount the vines on the board so they resemble a watermelon patch. Display the title of the board on a welcome sign. After each child makes a watermelon (see below), attach it to the patch.

Wonderful Watermelon

Supplies:
green construction paper oval (watermelon)
6" x 9" piece of green construction paper
cotton swab
green crepe paper
green paint
markers
scissors
glue or tape

Steps:
1. Use the cotton swab to paint green stripes on the watermelon.
2. Make a green handprint on the 6" x 9" piece of paper. When the paint is dry, use a marker to outline the handprint. Then trim around the tracing to make a leaf.
3. Use a marker to write your name on the leaf.
4. Tape or glue your leaf to a length of crepe paper and attach it to your watermelon.

Invite each child to use craft supplies to decorate a snorkeler cutout (pattern on page 125) so it resembles herself. Help each child write her name on her completed project; then post the projects on a board. Add lengths of twisted green crepe paper (seaweed) to complete the display.

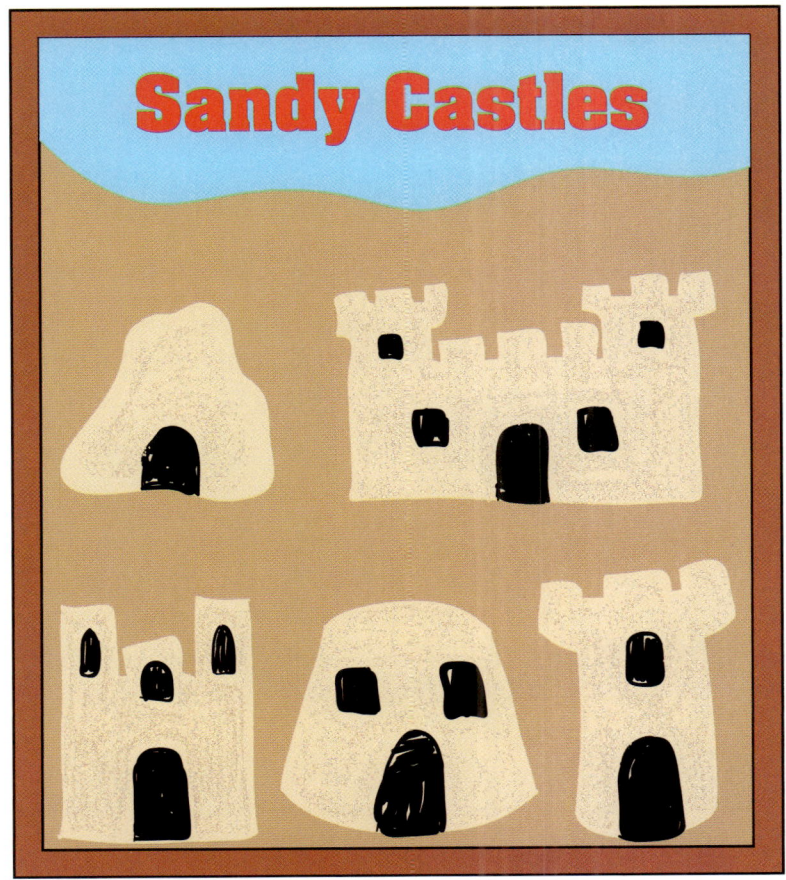

Help each child cut out a sand castle shape from a sheet of tan construction paper. Invite her to use a black crayon to add details, such as windows or a door. Then have her brush diluted glue on the castle (avoiding the added details) and sprinkle sand on the glue. After the glue dries, showcase students' sandy creations on a beach-themed board.

Little ones create an undersea paradise with this add-on display! Over several days, invite students to make different ocean critters (see below). As the creatures are completed, display them on a blue bulletin board paper ocean.

Sea Creatures

To make a lobster, brush diluted glue on a red lobster cutout (pattern on page 126) and sprinkle cornmeal on the glue.

To make a starfish, dot glue on a tan starfish cutout (pattern on page 127) and place O-shaped cereal pieces on the glue dots.

To make an octopus, sponge-paint a paper lunch bag. After the paint is dry, stuff the bag with newspaper to make a head and secure it with a length of yarn. Add facial features; then cut the bottom of the bag into eight strips and fold the strips up to make the octopus's legs.

Serve up some math practice with this cool graphing display. Use yarn to make four rows on a board. Label each of four blank cards with a different ice cream flavor. Post one card in each row. Have each youngster choose her favorite from the posted flavors and color an ice cream scoop cutout (pattern on page 128) to match. Help each child attach her scoop to the board in the corresponding row. Finally, discuss the results of the graph with the group. Incorporate the words *more, fewer, most, least,* and *equal* as appropriate.

Variations

- **A Tasty Treat!**
  Invite each youngster to create a new ice cream flavor and to decorate an ice cream scoop to show what it would look like. Attach the scoop to a cone cutout. Ask each child to name her ice cream flavor as you write it on her cone.

- **It's Been a "Scooper" Year**
  Have each child draw his favorite memory from the school year on an ice cream scoop cutout. Post the completed scoops in a large ice cream dish cutout.

Attach a red and white checkered tablecloth to a board. Have each child draw on a paper plate a picture of his favorite food. Label each plate with the name of the food and the child's name. Then attach the plates to the tablecloth. To complete the display, mount student-colored ant cutouts (pattern on page 128) on the tablecloth.

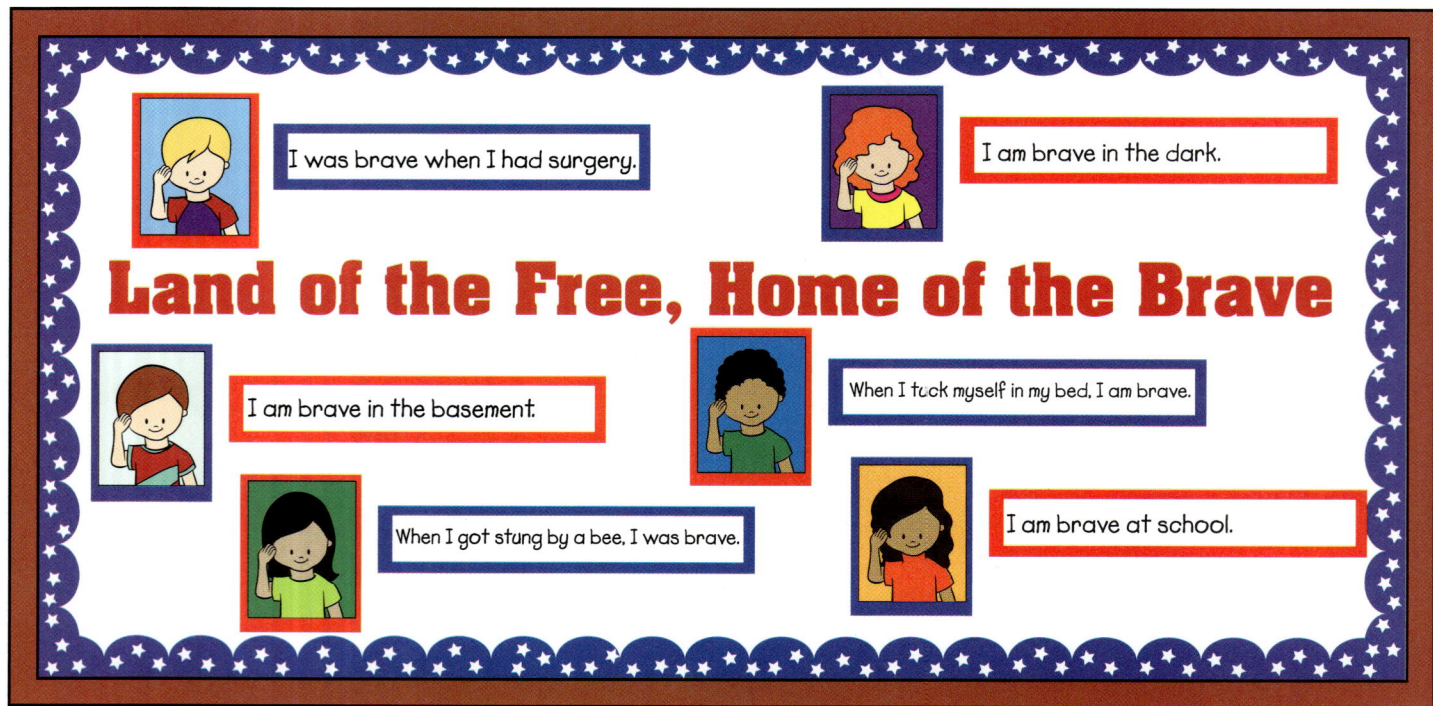

This patriotic display spotlights students' bravery. In advance, snap a photo of each child saluting. After a class discussion about bravery, ask each child to tell you about a time he was brave. List each child's response on a separate paper strip and post each child's photo near his strip.

Anytime Cooperation Quilt

Encourage cooperation and teamwork by making a class quilt! To make a quilt, mount a class supply of colorful construction paper squares on a large sheet of bulletin board paper. Invite a few youngsters at a time to the quilt. Designate a different square for each child and instruct each student to use art materials to decorate his square. After all of the pieces are complete, add a border. If desired, add a picture of each child to his square. Hang the completed class quilt on a wall to display this cooperative effort!

Here's a simple way to make a community display. Encourage little ones to name different places and objects in their communities. Then have each child use art materials to create a place or an object. Post the completed projects on a board decorated like the one shown. To complete the board, add child-colored vehicles (patterns on page 129).

Prompt students to use their thinking skills. Invite each child to decorate a bear cutout (pattern on page 130). When each bear is complete, staple it to a board so the body can be lifted up. To use the display, secretly tape a picture or a symbol on the board behind a bear. Then give youngsters clues so they can try to guess what the item is. When the correct answer is given, invite the owner of the bear to lift it up to reveal the item underneath!

Reinforce little ones' understanding of why it is important to keep clean with this bubbly display! Post a large bathtub cutout on a bulletin board. Invite each child to make a colorful bubble (see below). Then ask her to tell you why it is important to take a bath. After recording each child's response on the bathtub, post her bubble above the tub.

Colorful Bubble

Supplies:
milk
several colors of food coloring
small plastic cups
coffee filter
straw

Setup:
Fill several cups about half full with milk. Tint each cup of milk with a different color of food coloring.

Steps:
1. Place a flattened coffee filter on a covered surface.
2. Place one of the cups atop the filter.
3. Gently blow into the mixture with a straw until the bubbles flow over the top of the cup and down onto the filter.
4. Repeat Steps 2 and 3 with different colors until a desired effect is achieved.

The Alphabet Tree

After reading the book *Chicka Chicka Boom Boom* by Bill Martin Jr. and John Archambault, post a simple poster board palm tree on a wall. Each time you introduce a new letter, post it on the tree. Use the display to reinforce the new letters and to review the alphabet.

Variations

- **Matching Coconuts!**
  Program each of several brown circles (coconuts) with a different symbol—such as a letter, number, or shape—to make matching pairs. Randomly attach the coconuts to the tree with Sticky-Tac. Ask a student to find a matching pair. When he finds a match, he removes the coconuts from the tree and sets them to the side. Continue having students take turns in this manner until all of the matching pairs have been found.

- **Place the Coconut**
  A student attaches a coconut to the display according to a corresponding positional direction, such as "Put the coconut beside the tree" or "Put the coconut above the *A*."

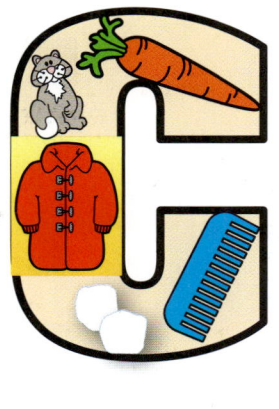

Reinforce letter recognition and beginning sounds with this take-home activity. Give each child a cardboard letter cutout to take home. Also send a note asking his parent to help him decorate the letter using different materials, objects, or pictures that begin with that letter and then to return the completed project to school. Any letters not sent home can be decorated as a class activity. After all letters have been completed, mount them in alphabetical order on a wall for a unique alphabet display.

Students get plenty of motivation to write when they make classroom mailboxes! Invite each child to color and cut out a tagboard mailbox (pattern on page 131). Next, help each child use a brad to attach a flag cutout to her mailbox and then to glue a paper post to the back. To complete the mailbox, assist her in gluing a lunch bag with its flap facing out to the back. Trim any excess bag. Mount the completed projects on a board and invite each youngster to write a letter to slip in a classmate's mailbox!

For each child, puzzle-cut a Humpty Dumpty pattern (page 132). Assist him in assembling the resulting puzzle and then in gluing it to a 12" x 18" sheet of blue construction paper. Invite him to decorate his Humpty Dumpty with hat and boot cutouts (patterns on page 133). Mount the completed projects on a board along with a copy of the traditional nursery rhyme, adding as a final line, "But We Can!"

Counting is a real treat with this yummy display! Make a tagboard cookie jar and mount it on a board along with an enlarged copy of the mouse pattern on page 123. Cut out a supply of tagboard cookies (patterns on page 134). Attach the loop sides of several Velcro fasteners to the cookie jar and the hook side of a Velcro fastener to the back of each cookie. To use the display, announce a number. Invite a student to count out the corresponding number of cookies and then to attach them to the cookie jar. After verifying her answer, remove the cookies and announce a different number.

Use the mouse cutout again. See page 55.

Highlight students' matching skills with this display! Copy the transportation cards on page 135 on several colors of construction paper. Cut out the cards and randomly post them on a board. Repeat the chant, "I spy with my little eye [a car]," inserting a different mode of transportation each time. After ending each chant, invite youngsters to look on the board for the matching mode of transportation!

✓ Student Activities

- **Counting Colors:** Name a color, and then invite a student to count the cards that have the matching color. After verifying the number counted is correct, name a different color and invite another student to count.

- **Making Comparisons:** Choose two different types of transportation, and then invite a student to count the number in each set. Then lead youngsters to compare the sets to see which has more, which has less, or if they are equal.

There are more trains than motorcycles.

Our Work Is BRIGHT!

Show off youngsters' bright work with this simple display! Have each child decorate a copy of the work display pattern on page 136 so the student on the pattern looks like himself. Next, have him glue the pattern to the top of a 12" x 18" sheet of construction paper. Add students' work to the sheets and post the projects on a wall. Mount an enlarged copy of the sun pattern from page 121 with the work samples.

Use the sun cutout again. See page 53.

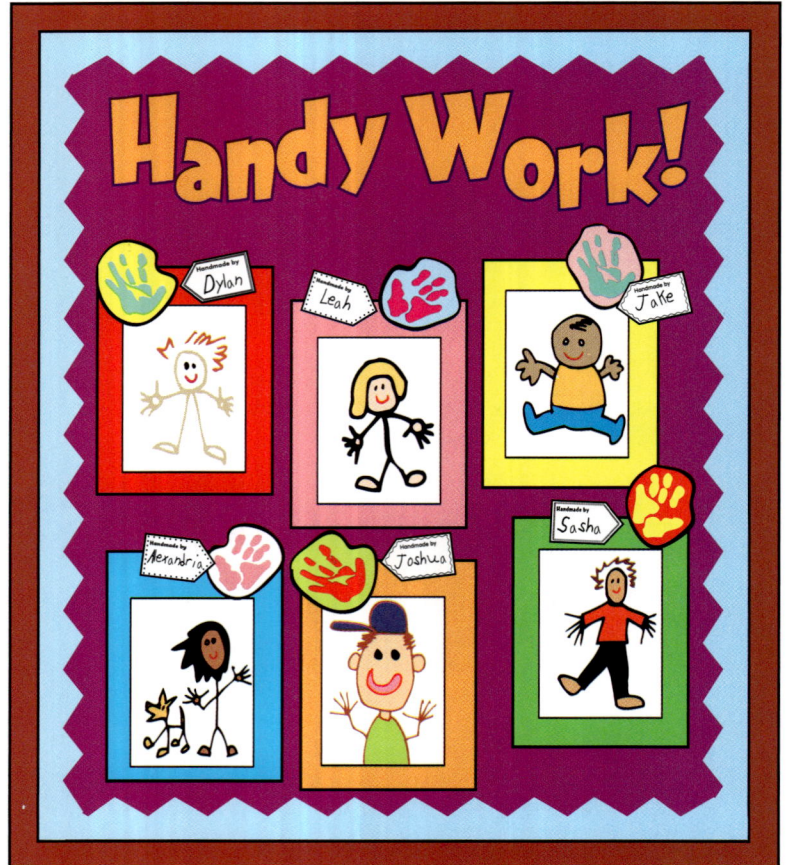

Invite each child to make a colorful handprint on a sheet of paper. After the paint dries, help him cut out his handprint and a copy of a tag pattern on page 136. Next, help him write his name on the tag and attach it along with his handprint to the top of a 9" x 12" sheet of construction paper. Mount the completed projects on a board and use them to showcase students' work!

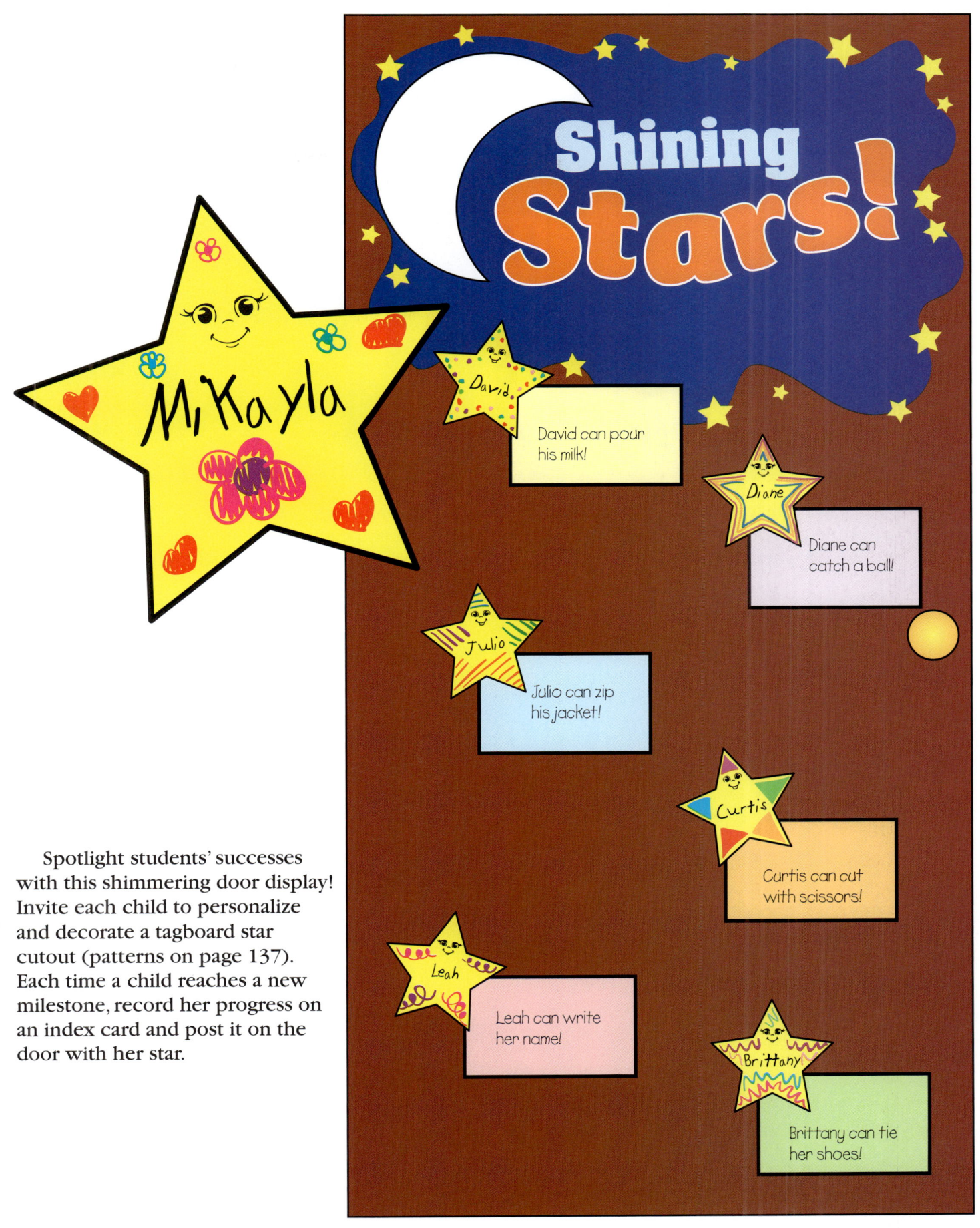

Shining Stars!

Spotlight students' successes with this shimmering door display! Invite each child to personalize and decorate a tagboard star cutout (patterns on page 137). Each time a child reaches a new milestone, record her progress on an index card and post it on the door with her star.

This board is the cat's meow on highlighting student work throughout the year! For each child, label a simple pawprint cutout with his name. Mount on a board each pawprint along with a corresponding work sample. Add an enlarged copy of the cat pattern on page 138 for a "purr-fect" display!

 ## Variations

- **Fall Is "Paws-itively" Terrific!**
  Post an enlarged copy of the rake pattern from page 139 next to the cat. Use the display to showcase students' finest fall work.

- **Winter Is "Paws-itively" Terrific!**
  Post an enlarged copy of the hat pattern from page 139 on the cat's head. Use the board to display little ones' wonderful winter work.

- **Spring Is "Paws-itively" Terrific!**
  Post an enlarged copy of the watering can pattern from page 139 on the cat's paw. Use the display to showcase students' springtime achievements.

- **Summer Is "Paws-itively" Terrific!**
  Post an enlarged copy of the sunglasses pattern from page 139 on the cat's head. Use the board to display youngsters' bright summer work.

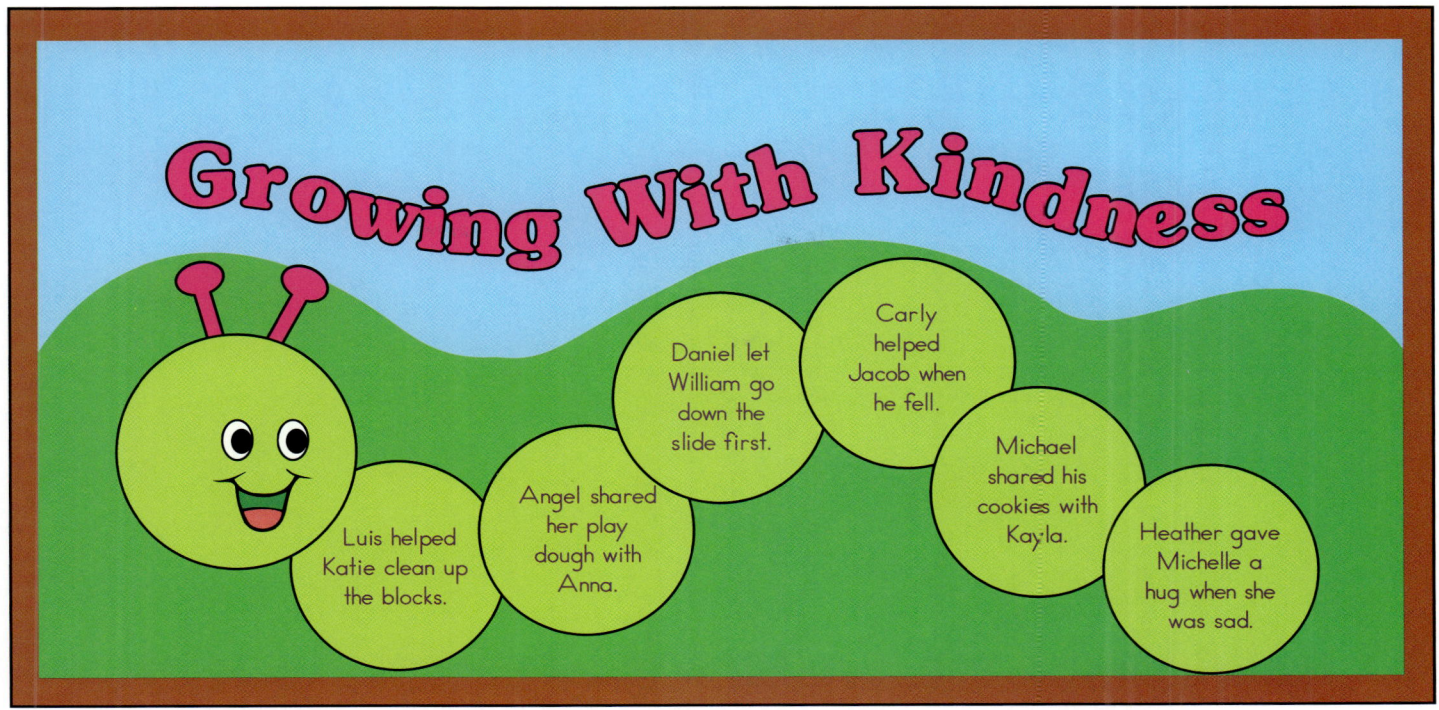

Good behavior helps this caterpillar grow! Cut out a supply of green construction paper circles. Decorate a circle to make the caterpillar's head and mount it on a board. Each time a student exhibits a kind behavior, record what she did on a circle and invite her to attach the circle to the caterpillar.

This display encourages your class to be on its best behavior. Post an enlarged copy of the gumball machine pattern on page 140. Obtain a supply of colorful dot stickers to use as gumballs. Each time the class displays a positive behavior, invite a child to add a sticky dot to the gumball machine. Once youngsters earn a predetermined number of gumballs, reward them with a treat or special privilege.

Feathered Friends

It's easy to keep track of your flock with this attendance display! After each child makes a paper-plate bird (see below), write her name on it and attach the hook side of a Velcro fastener to the back. Also attach for each child the loop side of a Velcro fastener to a large nest cutout. As each child arrives at school, she attaches her bird to the nest.

Paper-Plate Bird

Supplies:
white paper plate
colorful construction paper triangle (beak)
colorful pom-pom
colorful paint
paintbrush
glue

Setup:
Cut the plate into a bird shape.

Steps:
1. Paint the plate (bird).
2. Glue the beak to the bird.
3. Glue a pom-pom (eye) to the bird.

Keep students' paperwork organized and ready to send home with parents! Obtain a class supply of manila file folders and staple both sides of each folder; then label each folder with a child's name. Invite each child to decorate her prepared folder. Attach the folders to a wall for easy access. Post an enlarged copy of the elephant pattern on page 141 and a speech bubble with a reminder to parents as shown.

Cut out a large fishbowl from blue tagboard to make this handy helper chart. For an added touch, glue sandpaper to the bottom of the bowl. Label a separate fish cutout (patterns on page 76) for each classroom job and attach several to the bowl. For each child, personalize a tagboard circle (bubble). To assign jobs, use Sticky-Tac to attach a bubble next to each fish.

Crayon Patterns
Use with "A Brand-New Pack" on page 5.

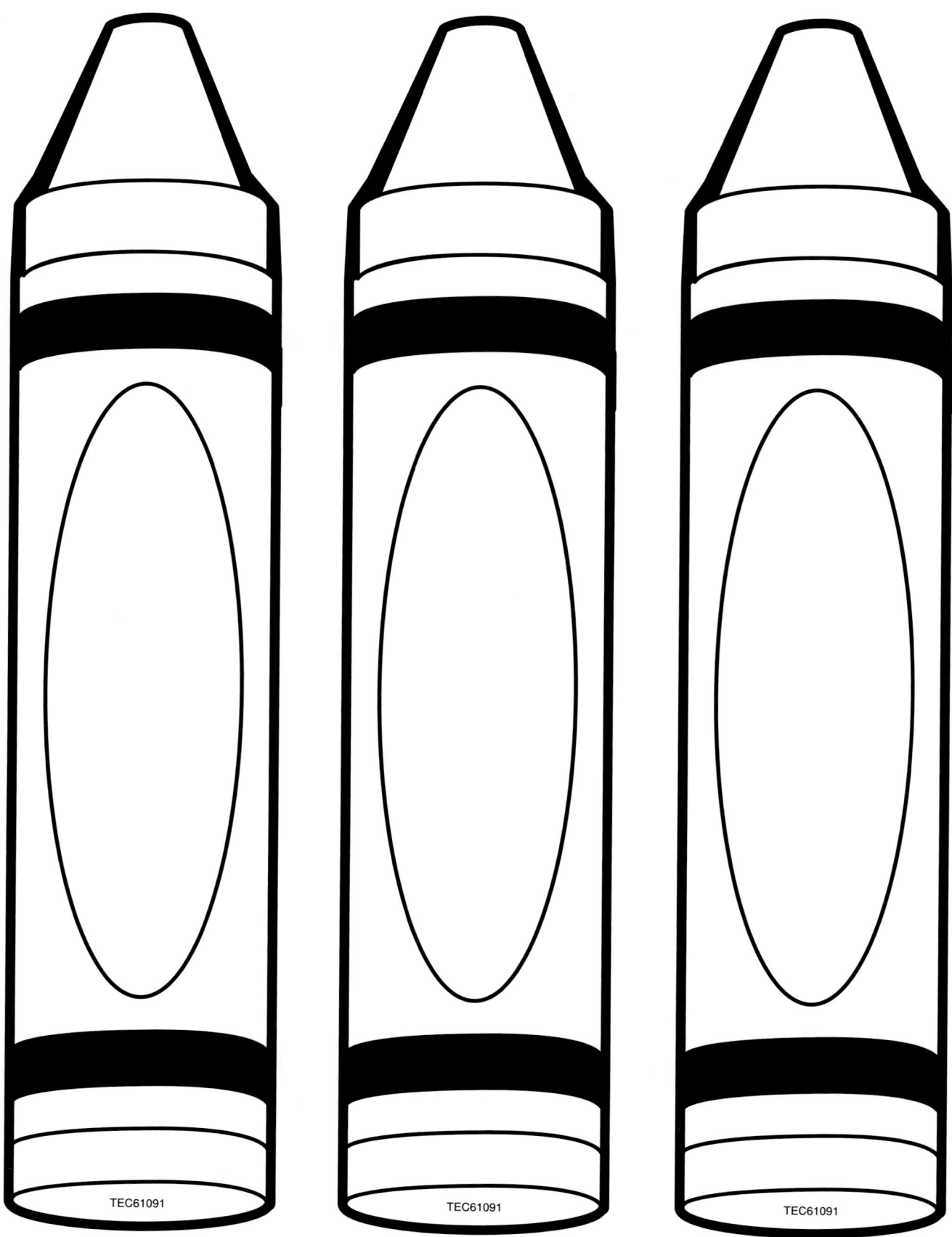

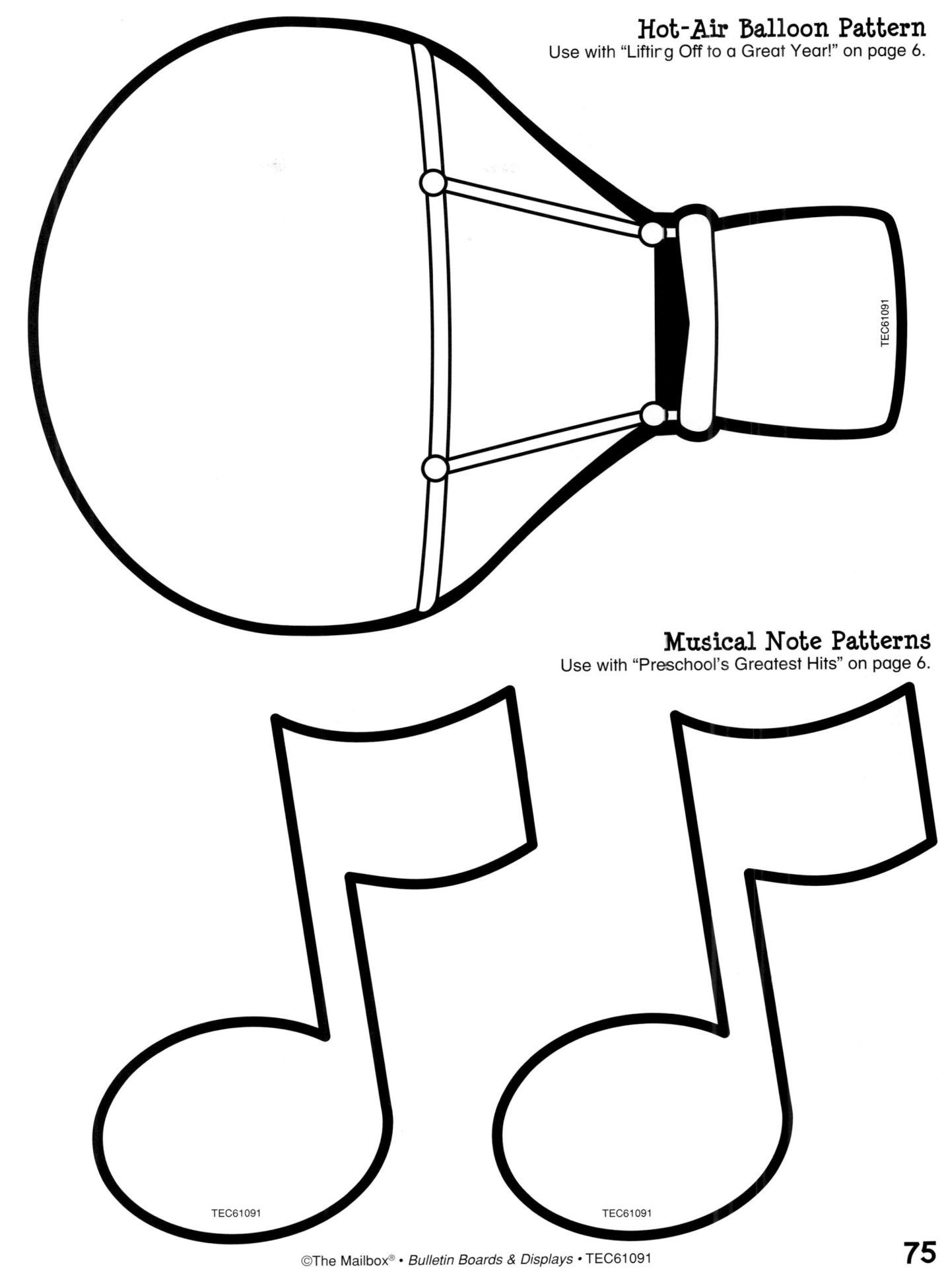

Hot-Air Balloon Pattern
Use with "Lifting Off to a Great Year!" on page 6.

Musical Note Patterns
Use with "Preschool's Greatest Hits" on page 6.

Fish Patterns
Use with "We Love Our School!" on page 8 and "A School of Helpers" on page 73.

Child Pattern

Use with "Circle of Friends" on page 9 and "Wrapped Up in Learning" on page 21.

Squirrel Pattern

Use with "We're Nuts About Starting Preschool!" on page 10, "A Hungry Squirrel" on page 17, and "Staying Warm This Winter!" on page 25.

Acorn Pattern

Use with "We're Nuts About Starting Preschool!" on page 10 and "A Hungry Squirrel" on page 17.

Hive Pattern
Use with "Busy Little Bees" on page 11.

Bee Patterns

Use with "Busy Little Bees" on page 11, "We've Been Busy Bees!" on page 16, and "'Bee' a Good Friend!" on page 48.

81

Duck Pattern
Use with "Who's the Helper of the Day?" on page 11.

Bow Patterns
Use with "High-Flying Helpers" on page 12.

Star Pattern
Use with "Birthday Stars" on page 13.

Wishing Well Pattern
Use with "Classroom Wishes" on page 14.

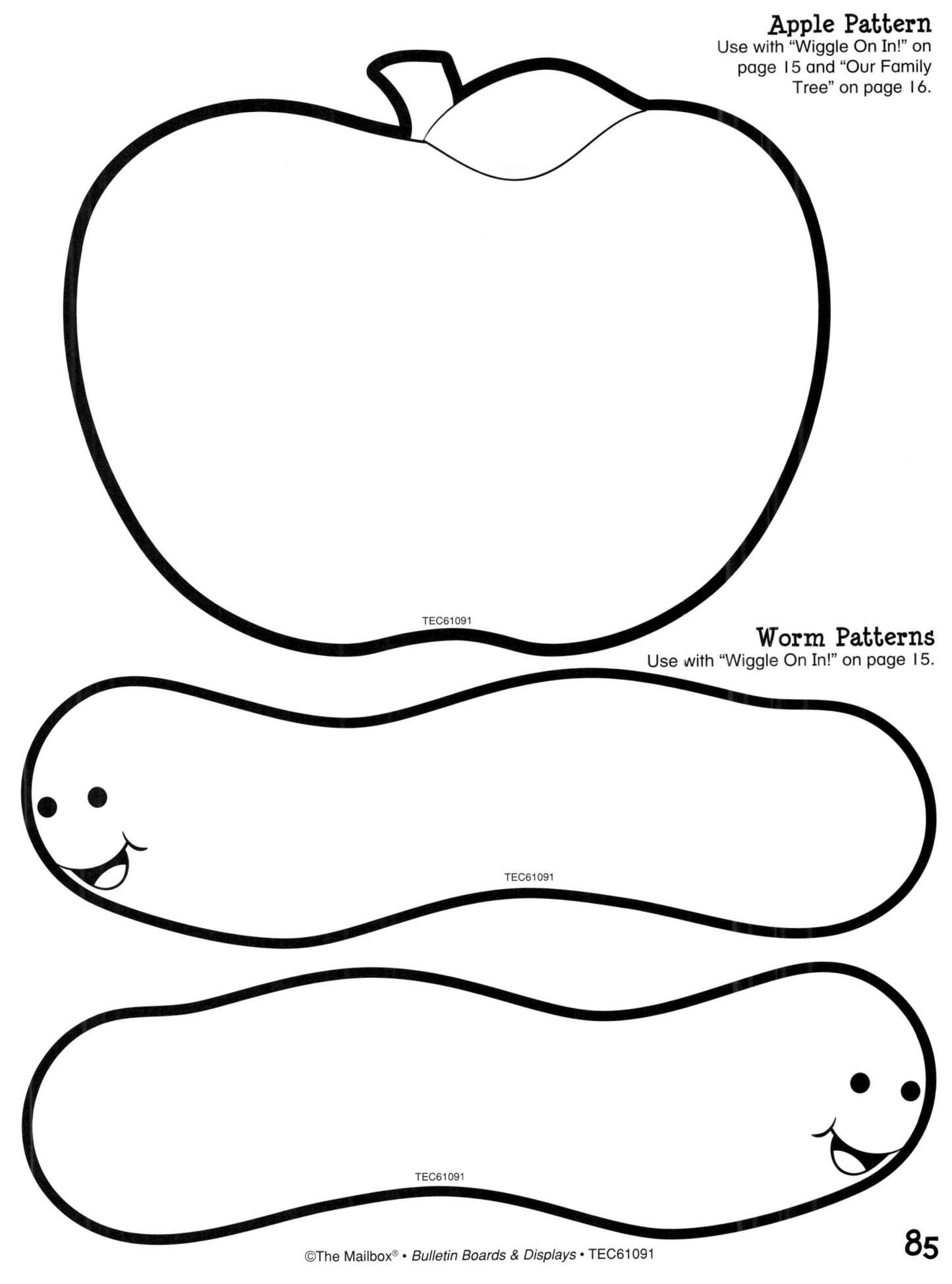

Leaf Patterns
Use with "Our Family Tree" on page 16 and "Falling Into Learning" on page 17.

Snowflake Patterns
Use with "Winter Wonderland" on page 16.

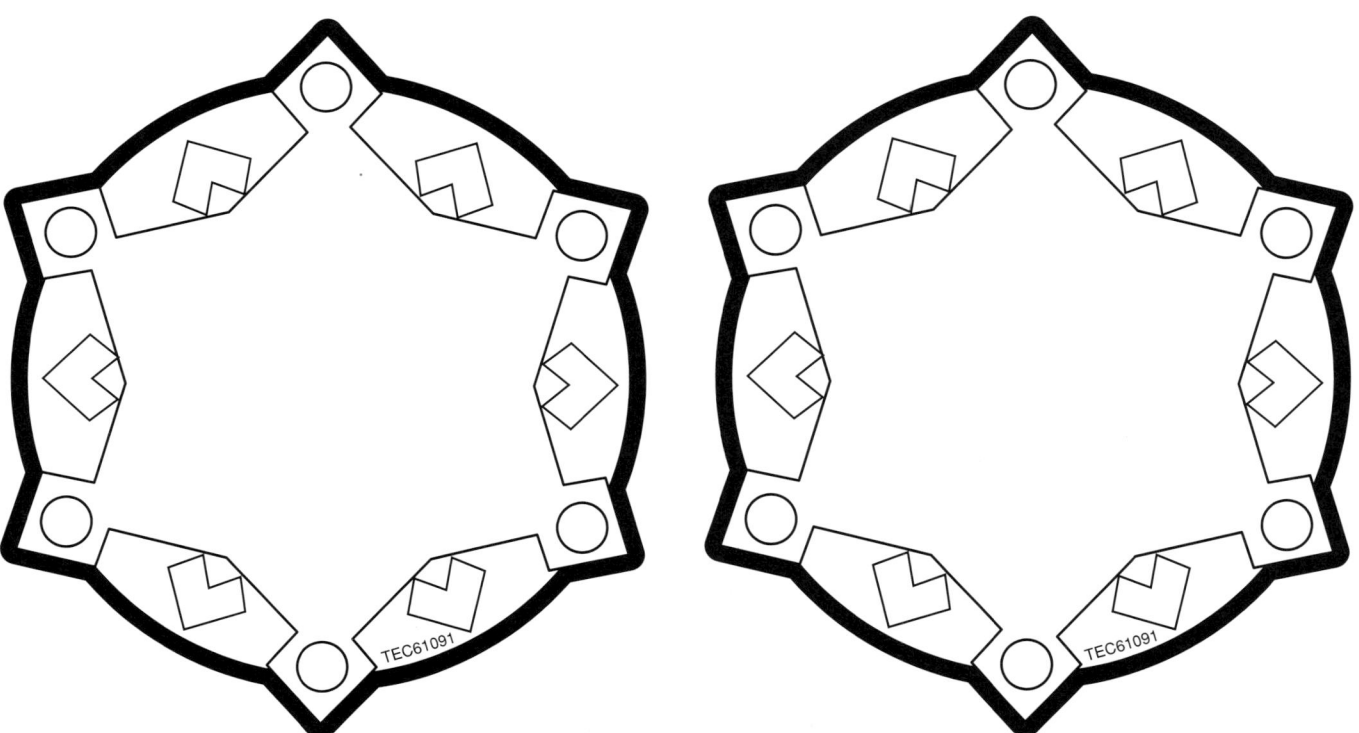

Scarecrow Pattern
Use with "A Harvest of Fun!" on page 18.

Dalmatian Pattern
Use with "Spotting Fire Safety Rules!" on page 19.

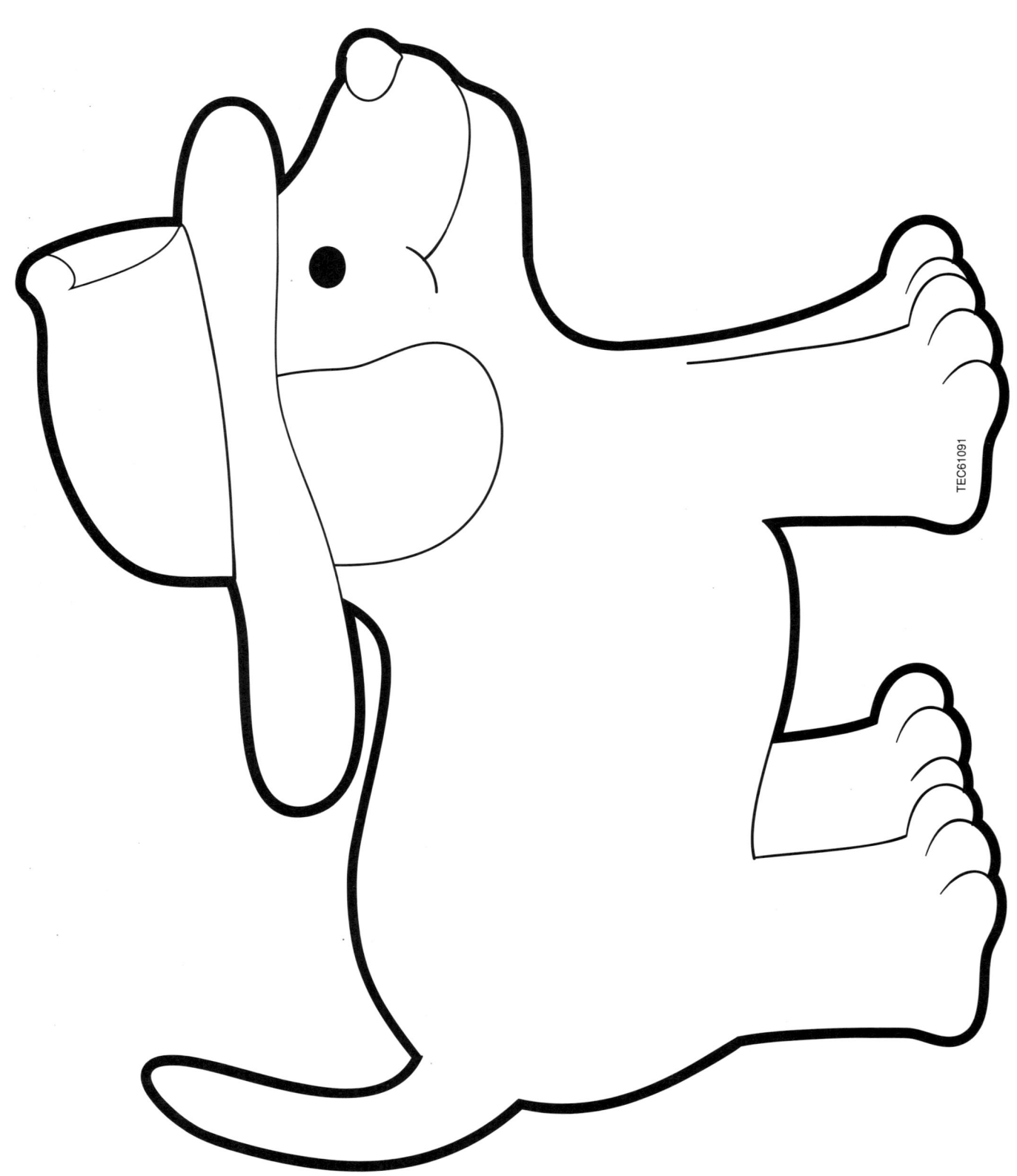

Pumpkin Pattern
Use with "Look Who's in the Pumpkin Patch" and "What's Inside of a Pumpkin?" on page 20.

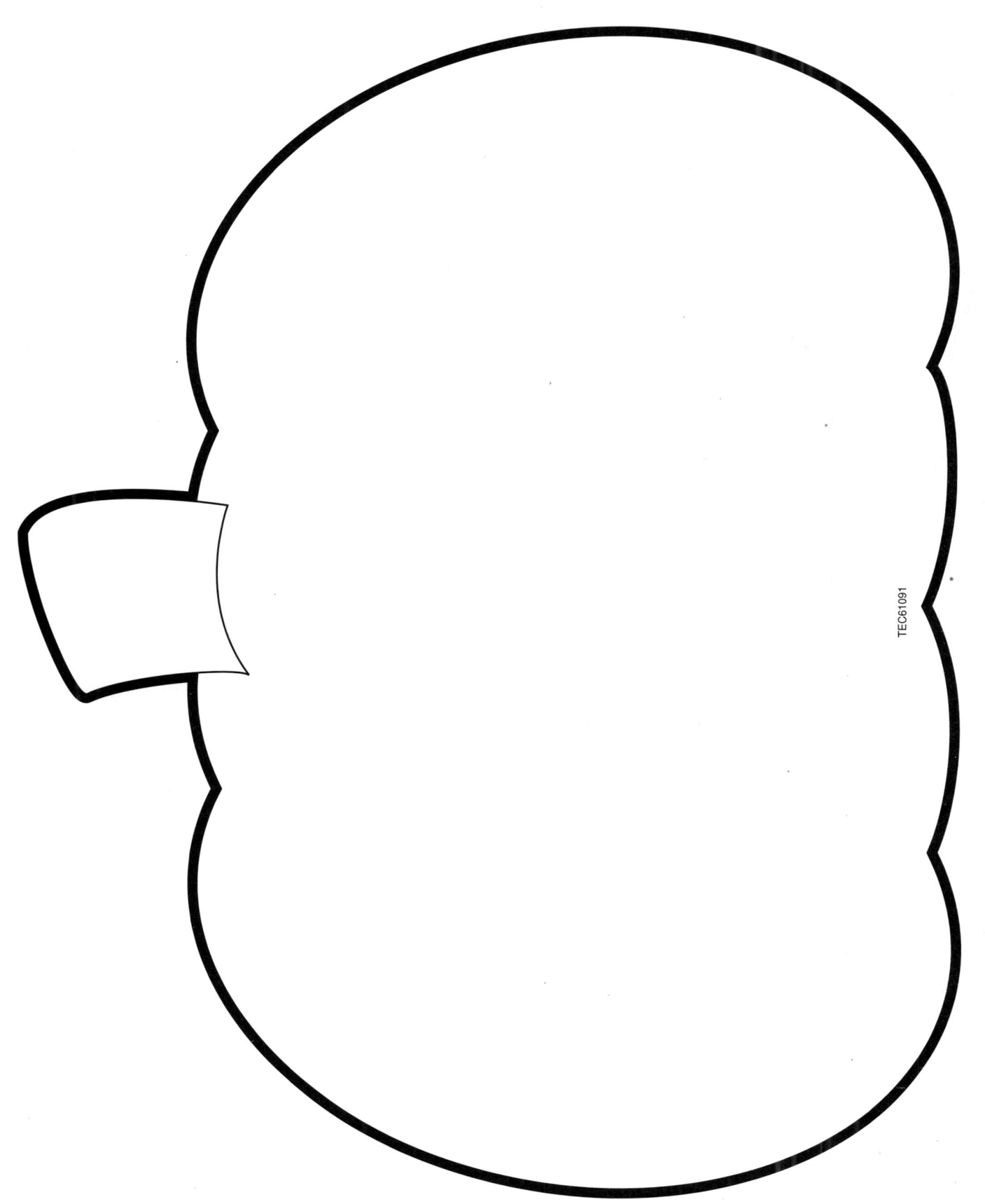

Tree Pattern
Use with "A Forest of Families" on page 22.

With my family, I like to

_____.

_____
name

With my family, I like to

_____.

_____
name

Note to the teacher: Use with "A Forest of Families" on page 22.

Turkey Head and Feet Patterns
Use with "Stuffed With Thankfulness" on page 23.

Feather Pattern
Use with "Stuffed With Thankfulness" on page 23 and "How Many Feathers?" on page 24.

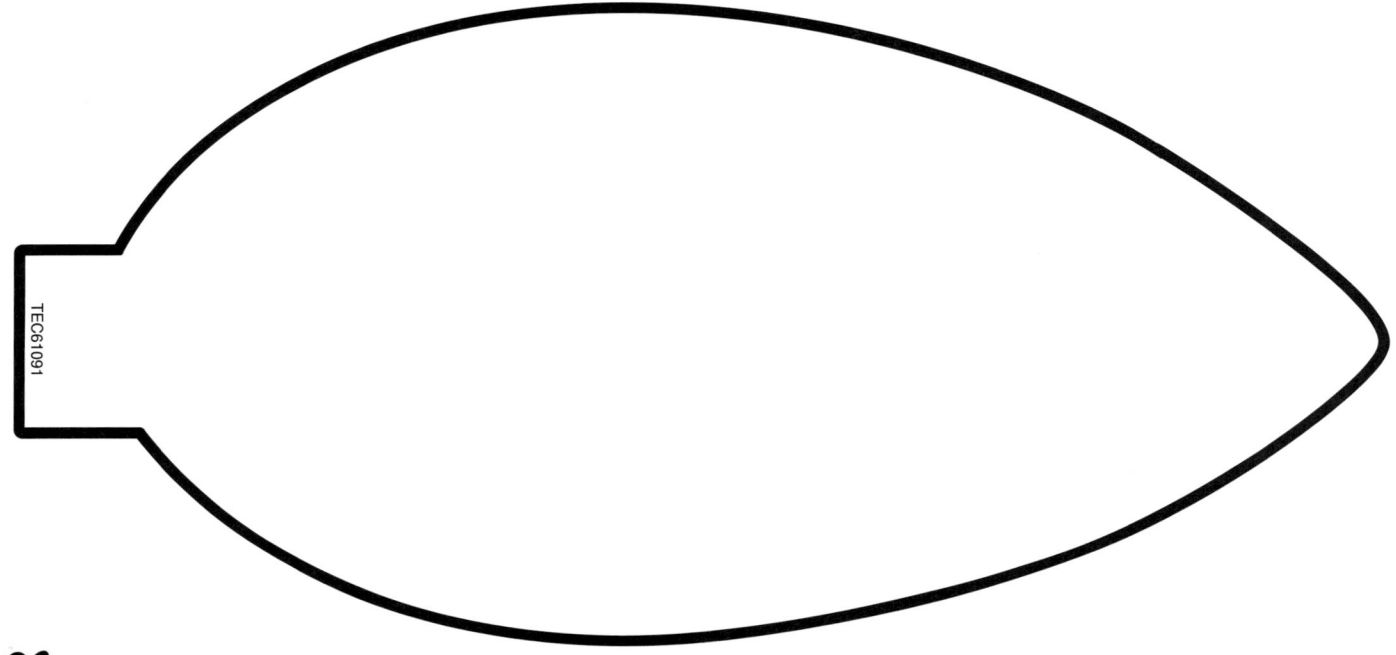

Turkey Pattern
Use with "How Many Feathers?" on page 24.

Winter Clothing Patterns
Use with "Staying Warm This Winter!" on page 25.

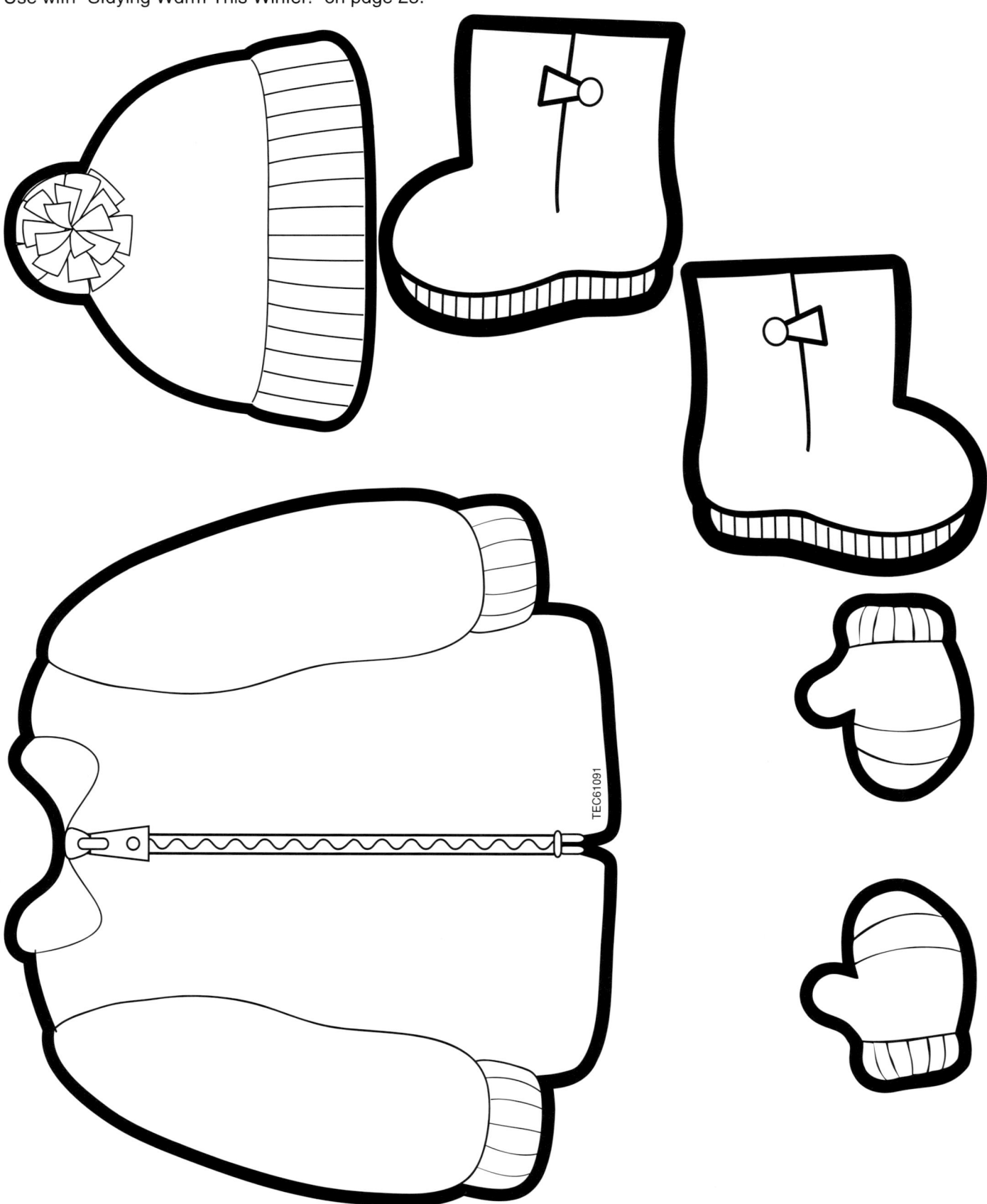

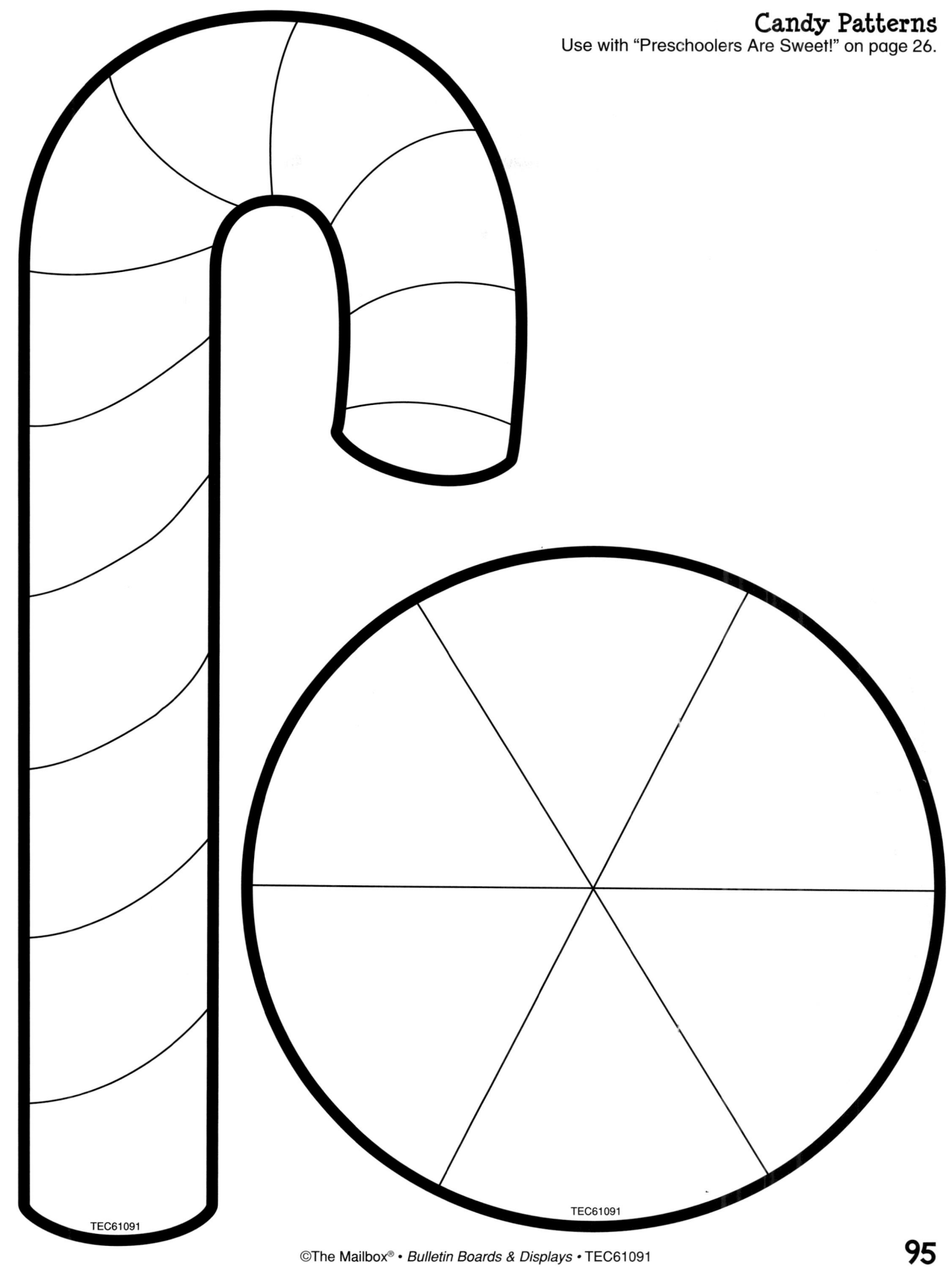

Candy Patterns
Use with "Preschoolers Are Sweet!" on page 26.

Gingerbread Cookie Patterns
Use with "Can't Catch Us!" on page 28.

Corn Patterns
Use with "A Kwanzaa Celebration!" on page 31.

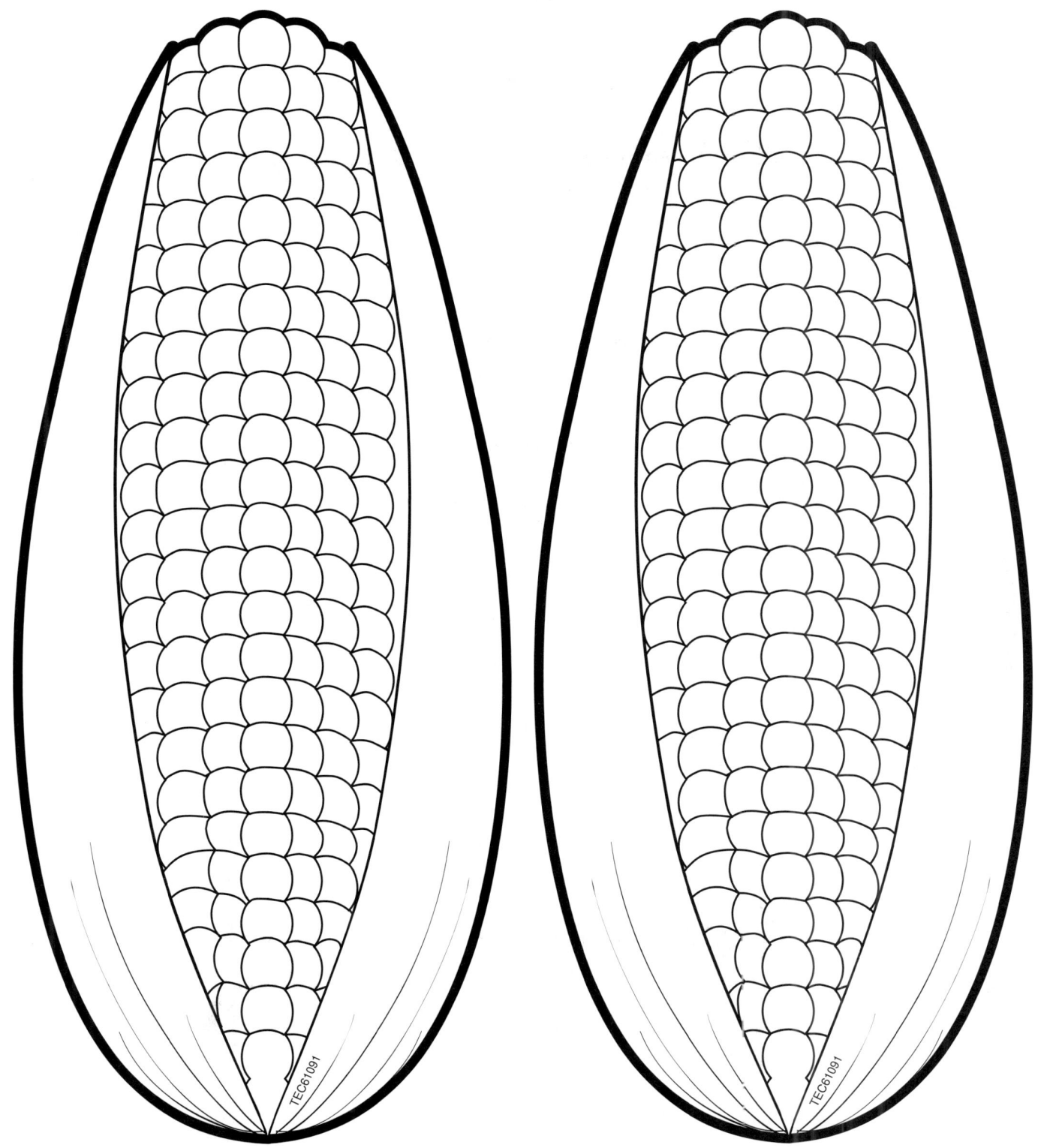

Engine Pattern
Use with "The Preschool Express" on page 31.

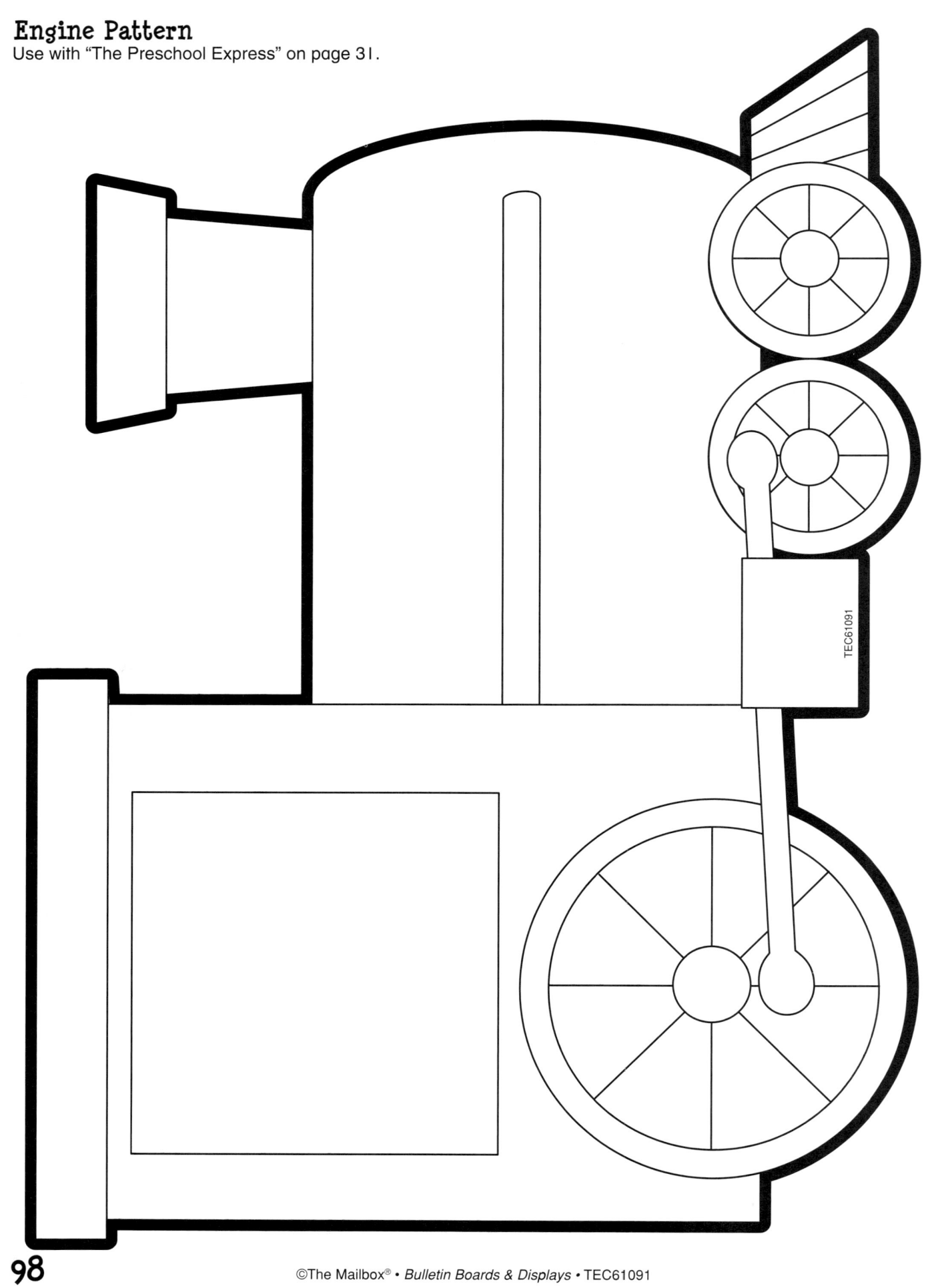

Boxcar Pattern
Use with "The Preschool Express" on page 31.

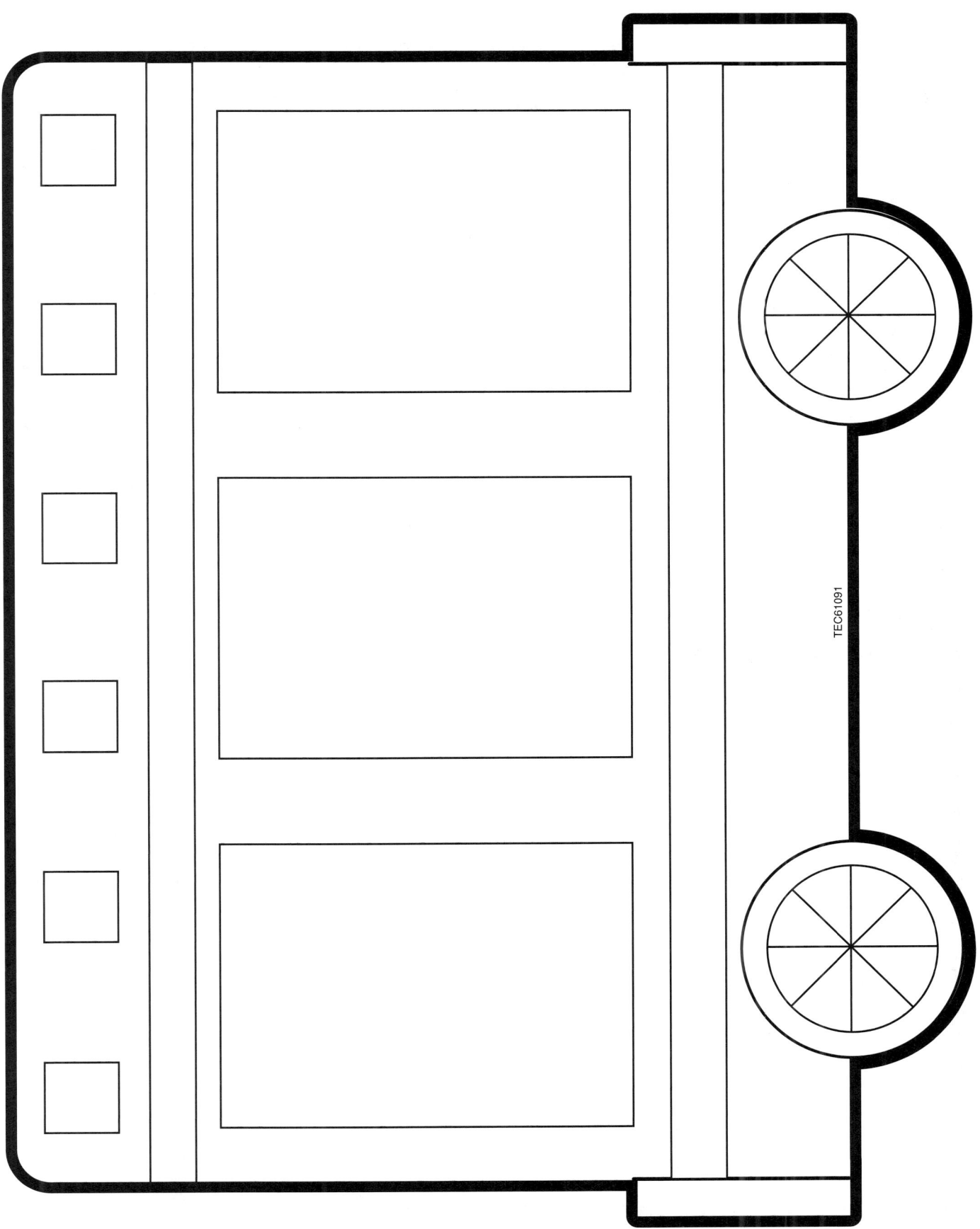

Mitten and Sock Patterns

Use with "Wishing You Warm Hands and Toasty Toes" on page 32.

100 ©The Mailbox® • Bulletin Boards & Displays • TEC61091

Penguin Pattern
Use with "All Dressed Up for the New Year!" on page 33.

©The Mailbox® • *Bulletin Boards & Displays* • TEC61091

101

Hat Patterns
Use with "All Dressed Up for the New Year!" on page 33 and "Snowpals on Ice!" on page 35.

Skate Patterns
Use with "Snowpals on Ice!" on page 35.

Bear Pattern
Use with "Polar Rhyme Time" on page 34.

Paw-Print Patterns
Use with "Polar Rhyme Time" on page 34.

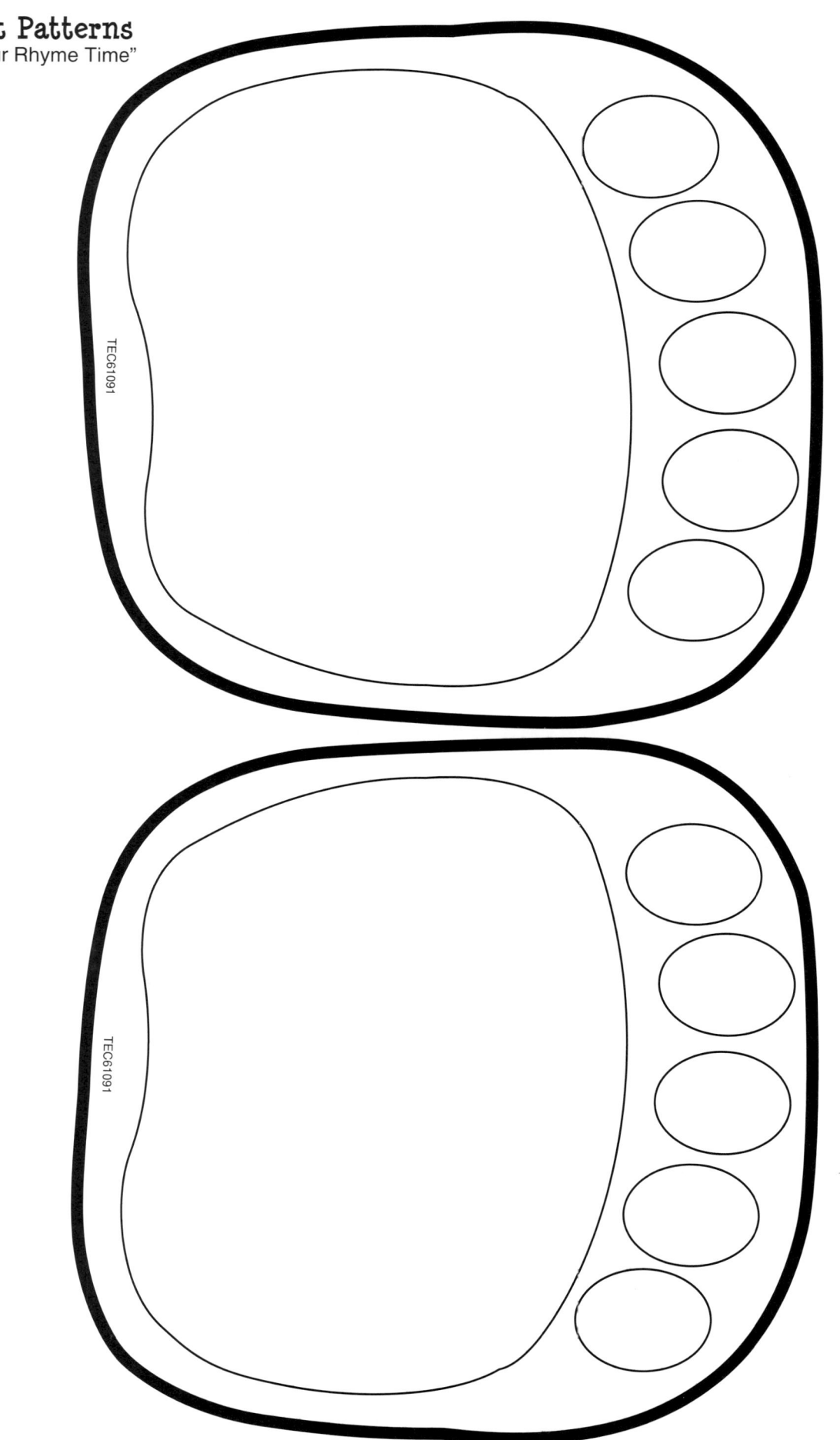

Groundhog Pattern
Use with "Shhhh! Groundhogs Napping" on page 36.

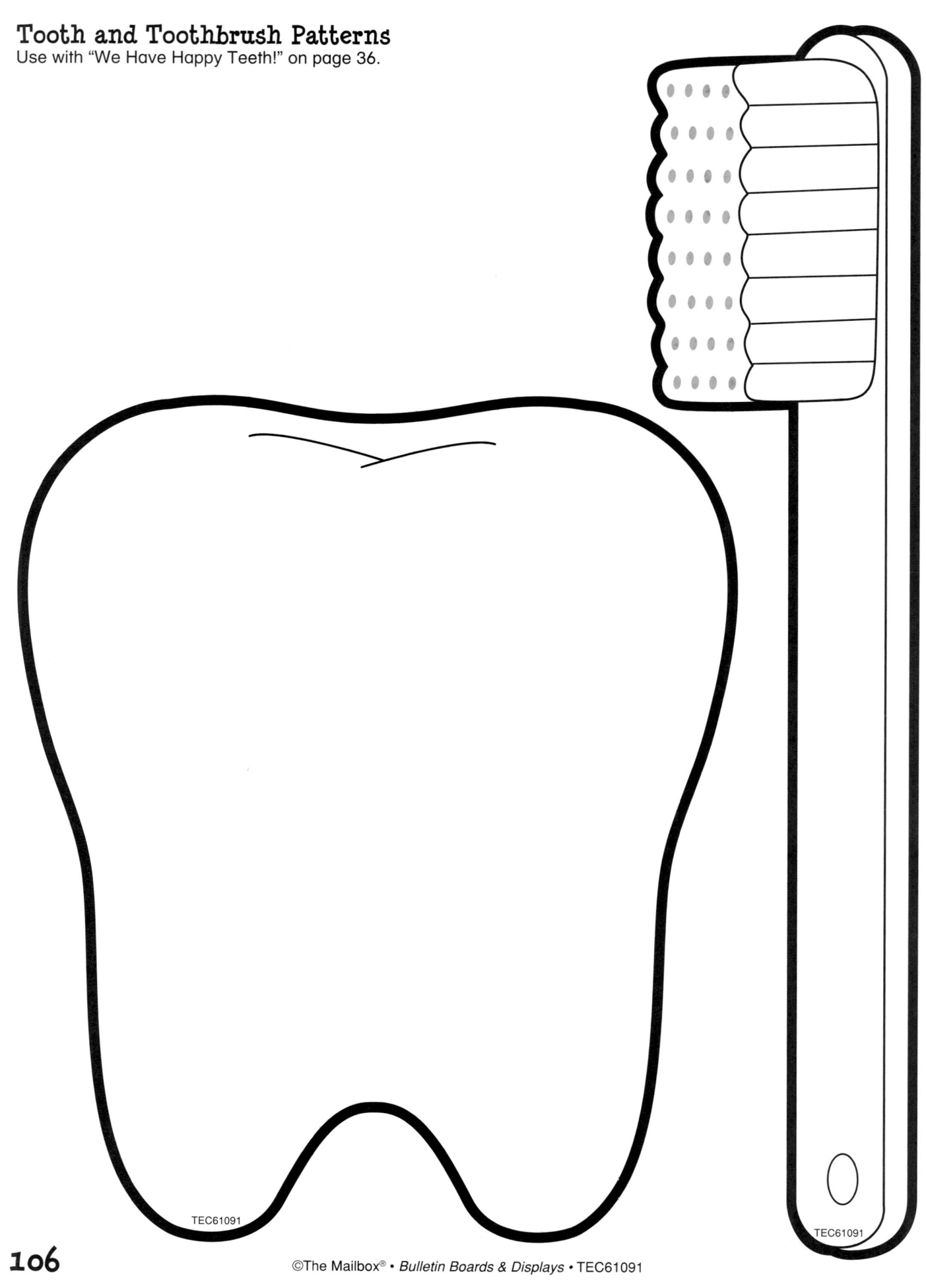

Egg and Ham Patterns and Recording Sheet
Use with "Green Eggs and Ham: Tasty or Not?" on page 39.

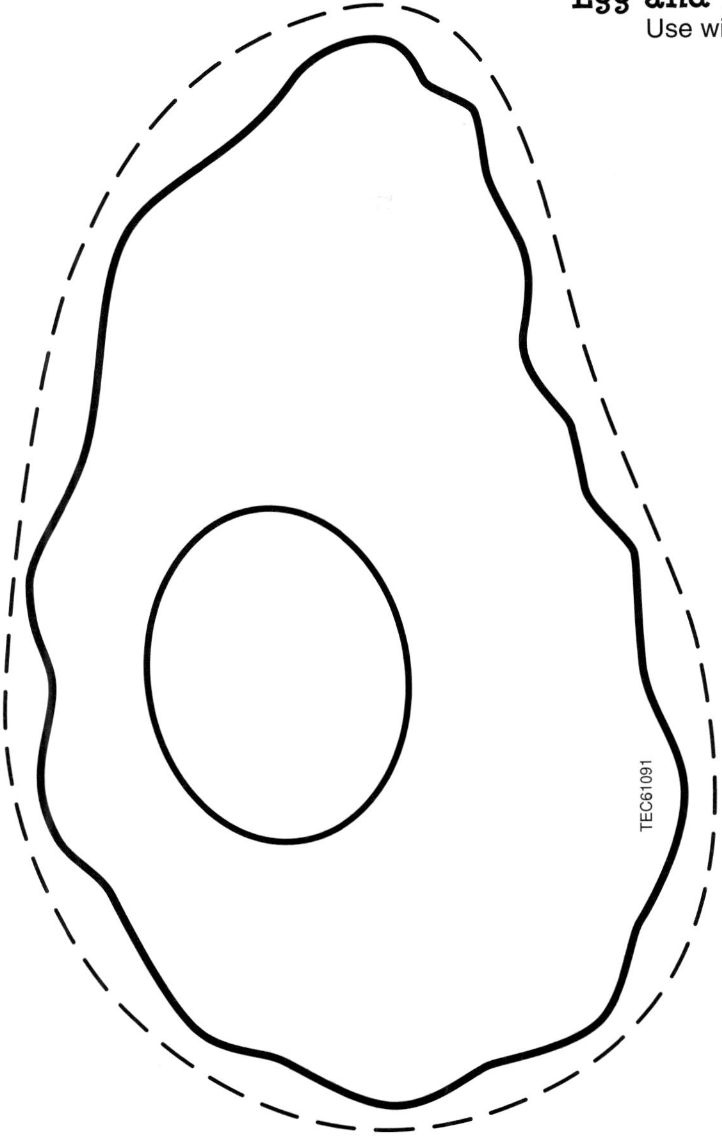

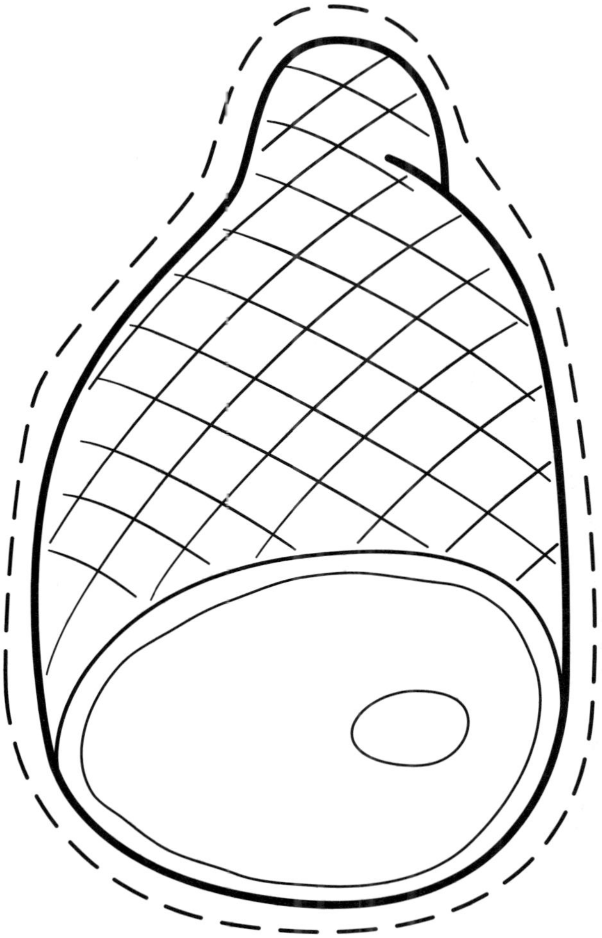

Would you like green eggs and ham?

yes   maybe   no

©The Mailbox® • Bulletin Boards & Displays • TEC61091

Shamrock Pattern
Use with "The Shamrock Showplace" on page 40.

Leprechaun Pattern
Use with "The Shamrock Showplace" on page 40.

Lamb Pattern
Use with "Little Lambs" on page 41.

110 ©The Mailbox® • Bulletin Boards & Displays • TEC61091

Barn Pattern
Use with "Little Lambs" on page 41.

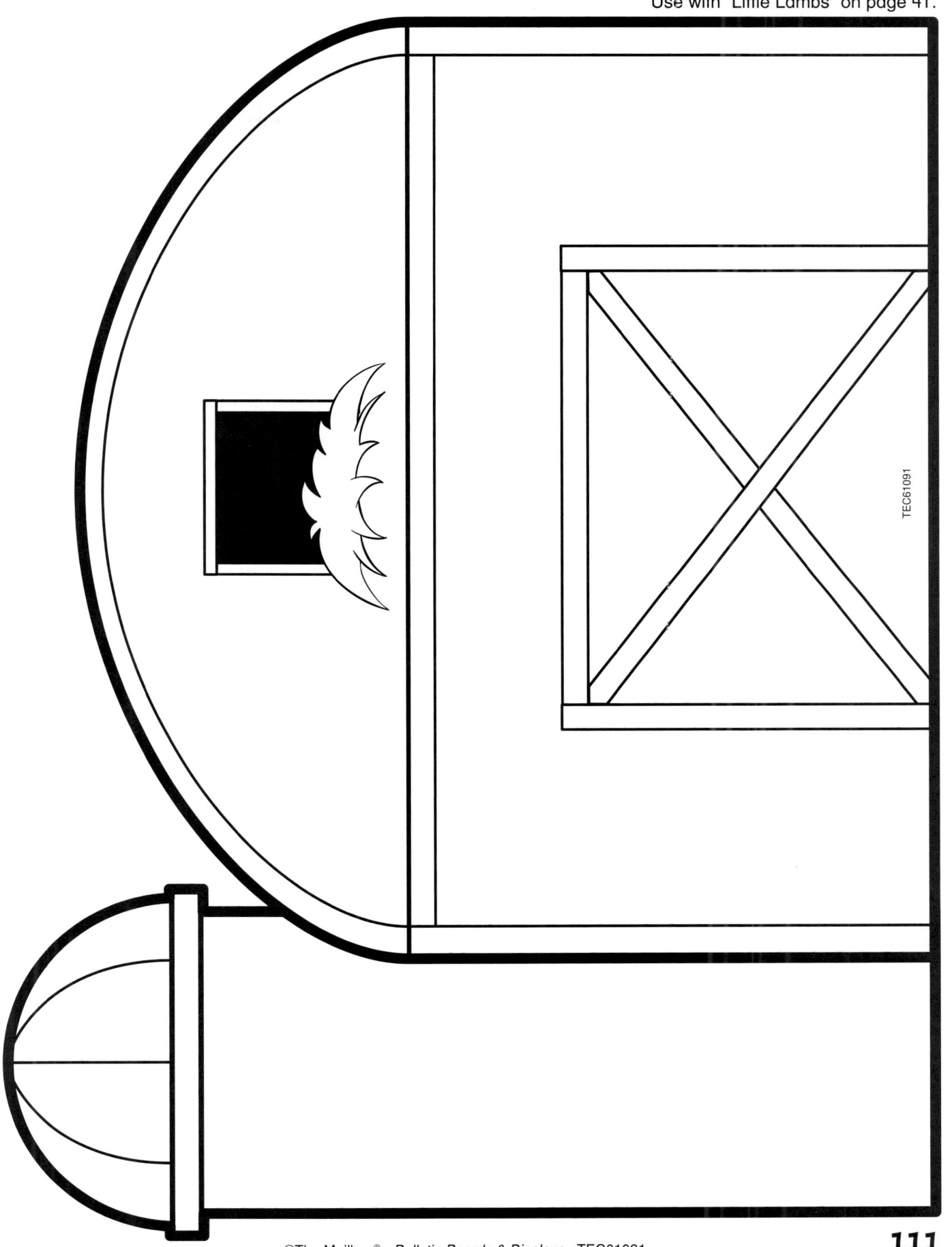

Raindrop Patterns
Use with "April Showers" on page 44.

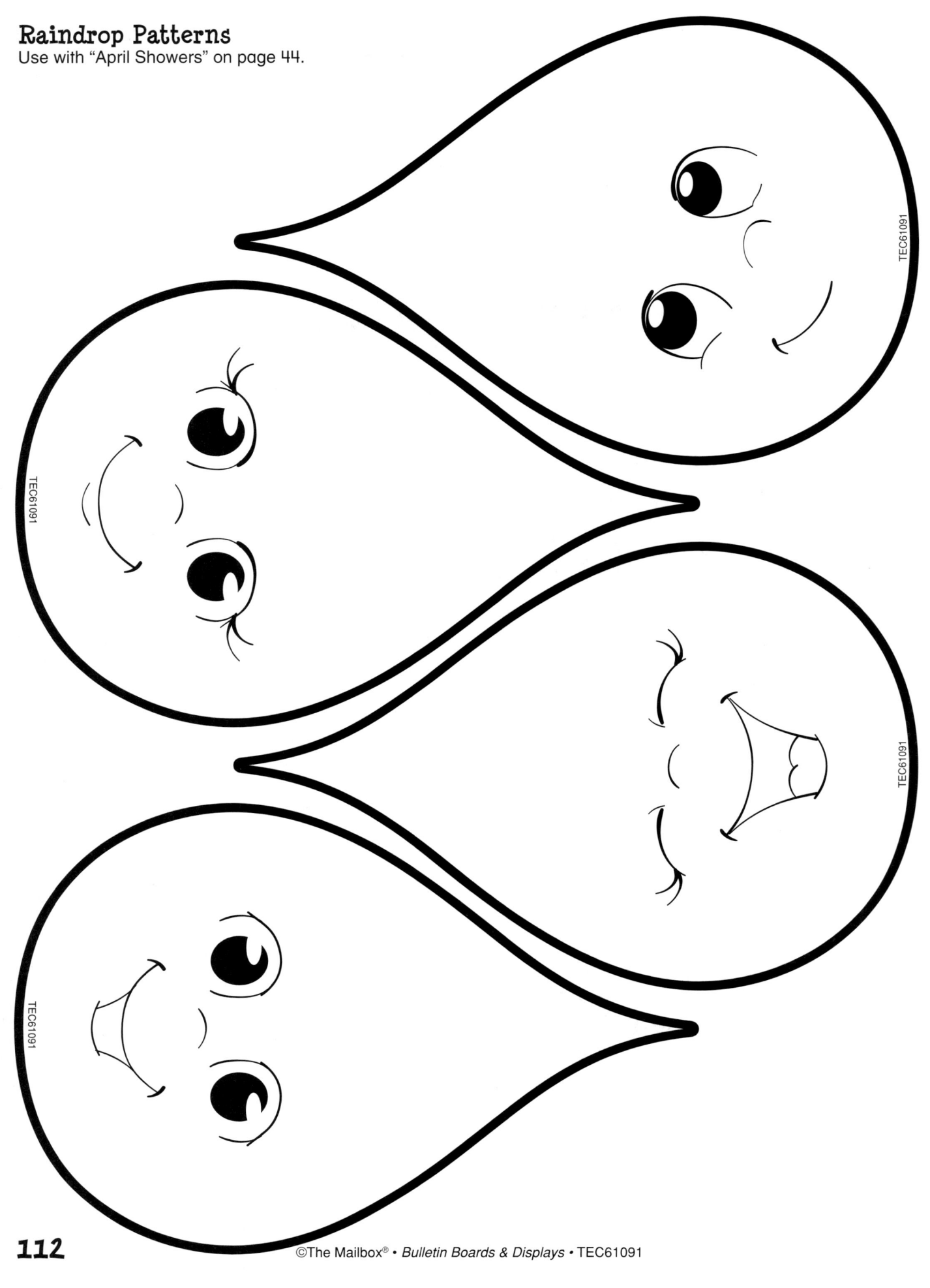

Pig Pattern
Use with "Fun in the Mud!" on page 44.

Ladybug Patterns
Use with "Ten Lovely Ladybugs" on page 45.

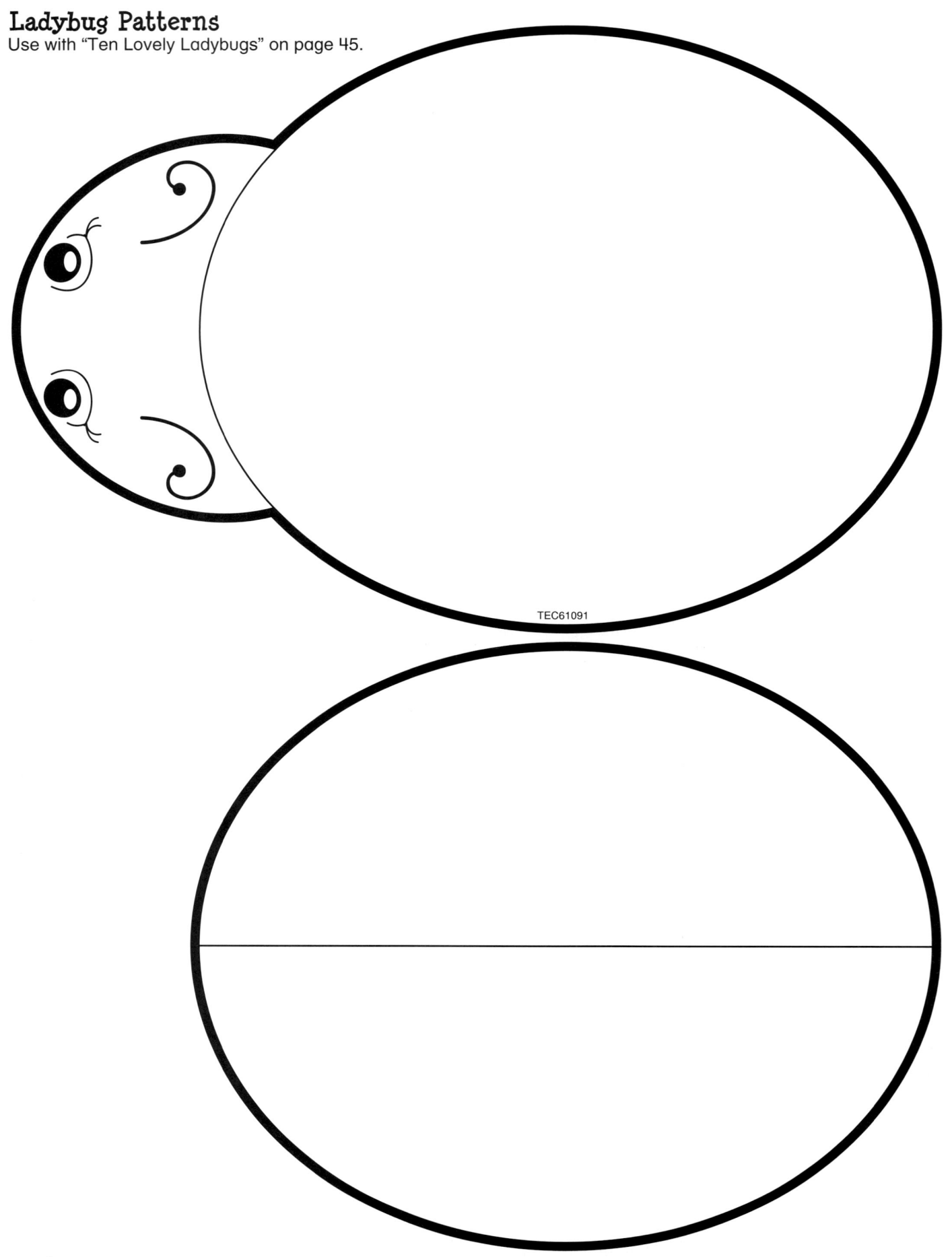

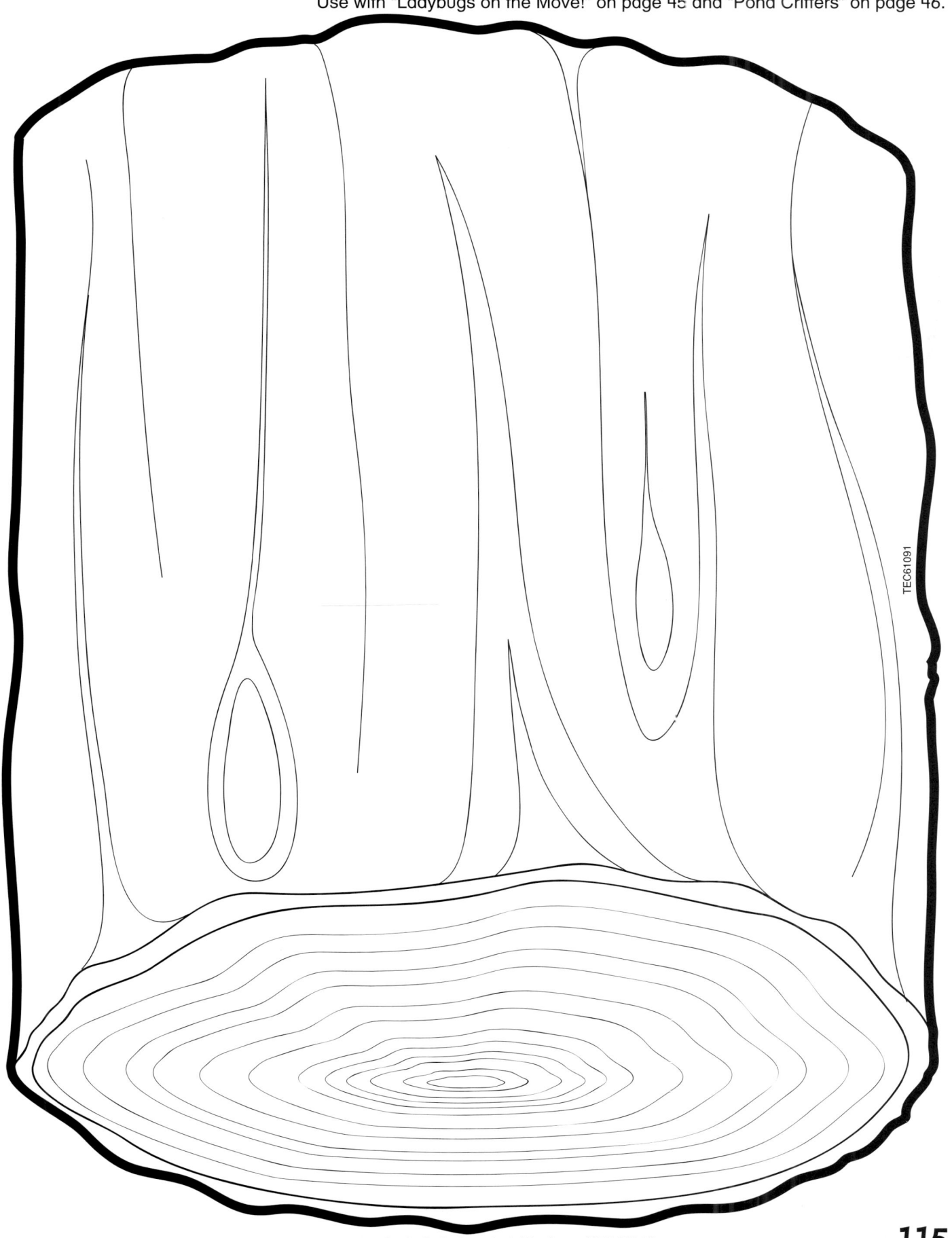
Log Pattern
Use with "Ladybugs on the Move!" on page 45 and "Pond Critters" on page 46.

Fish and Duck Patterns
Use with "Pond Critters" on page 46.

Turtle and Frog Patterns
Use with "Pond Critters" on page 46.

©The Mailbox • Bulletin Boards & Displays • TEC61091

Bee and Wing Patterns
Use with "Buzzing With Pride!" on page 49.

Sail and Boat Patterns
Use with "Sailing Into Summer!" on page 52.

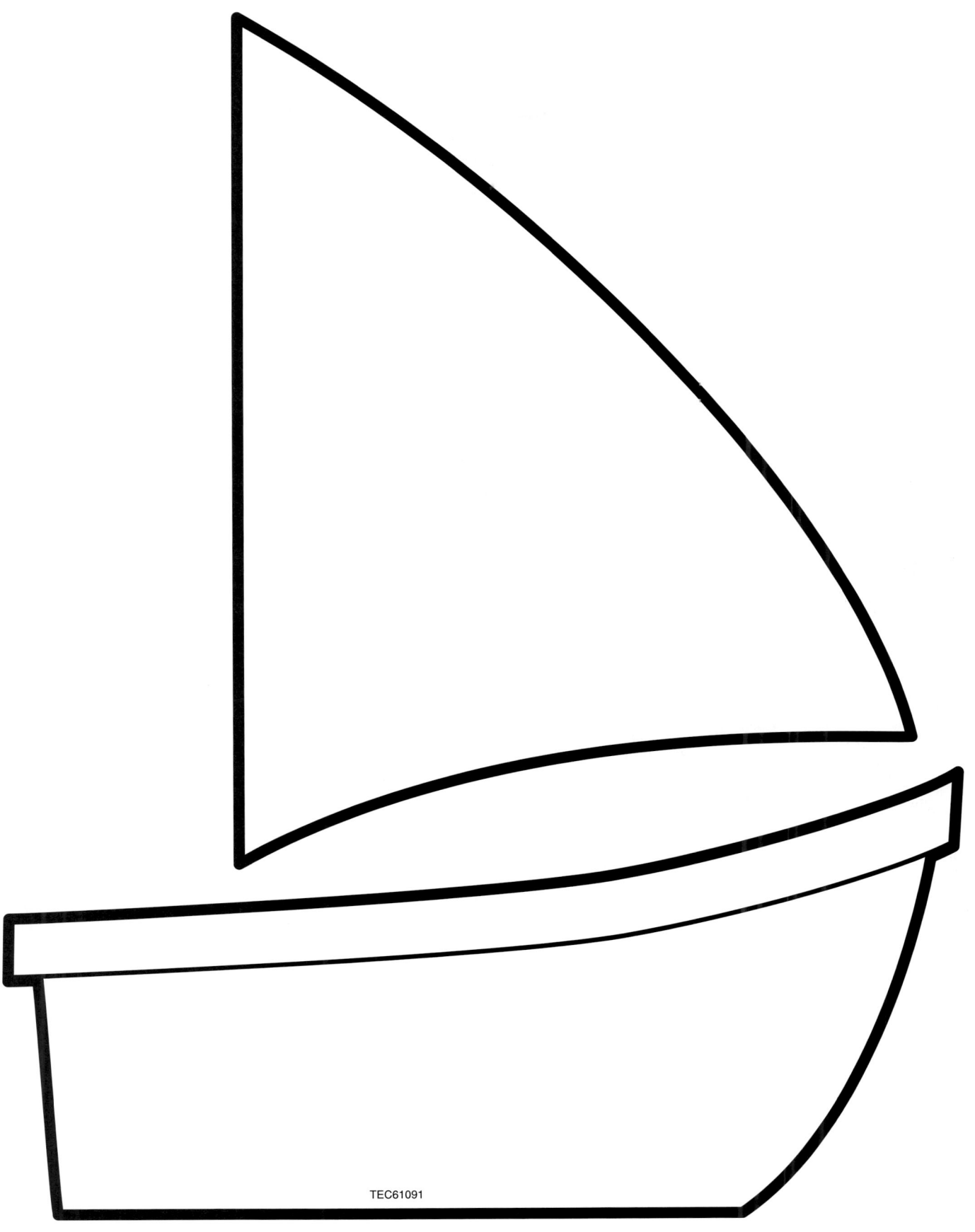

119

Puppy Pattern
Use with "Dandy Wishes" on page 53.

Sun Pattern

Use with "Our Future's So Bright, We've Got to Wear Shades!" on page 53 and "Our Work Is Bright!" on page 68.

Racecar Patterns
Use with "Racing to Kindergarten" on page 54.

Mouse Pattern
Use with "Berry Picking" on page 55 and "Freshly Baked!" on page 66.

©The Mailbox® • Bulletin Boards & Displays • TEC61091

123

Strawberry Patterns
Use with "Berry Picking" on page 55.

Snorkeler Pattern
Use with "Diving Into Summer" on page 57.

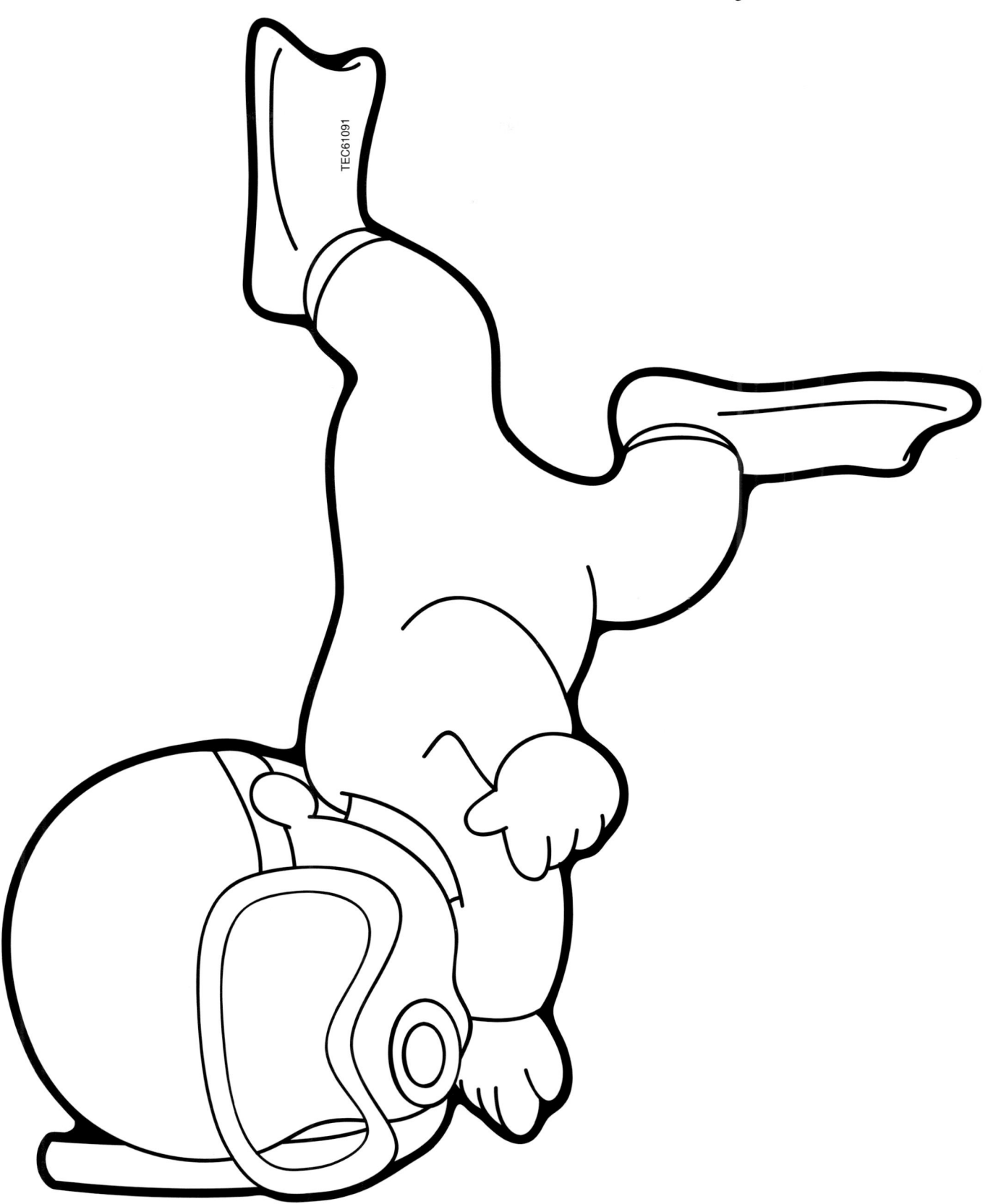

Lobster Pattern
Use with "Under the Sea" on page 58.

Starfish Pattern
Use with "Under the Sea" on page 58.

Ice Cream Scoop Pattern
Use with "Our Favorite Flavors" on page 59.

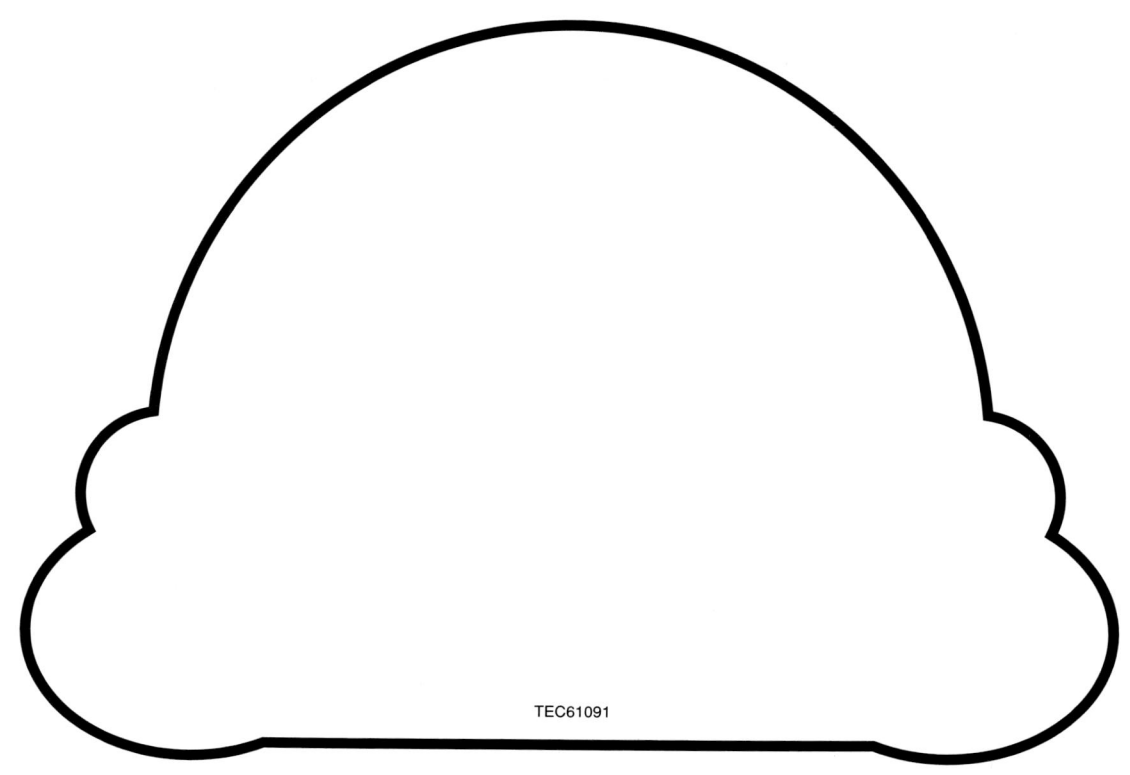

Ant Pattern
Use with "Our Preschool Picnic" on page 60.

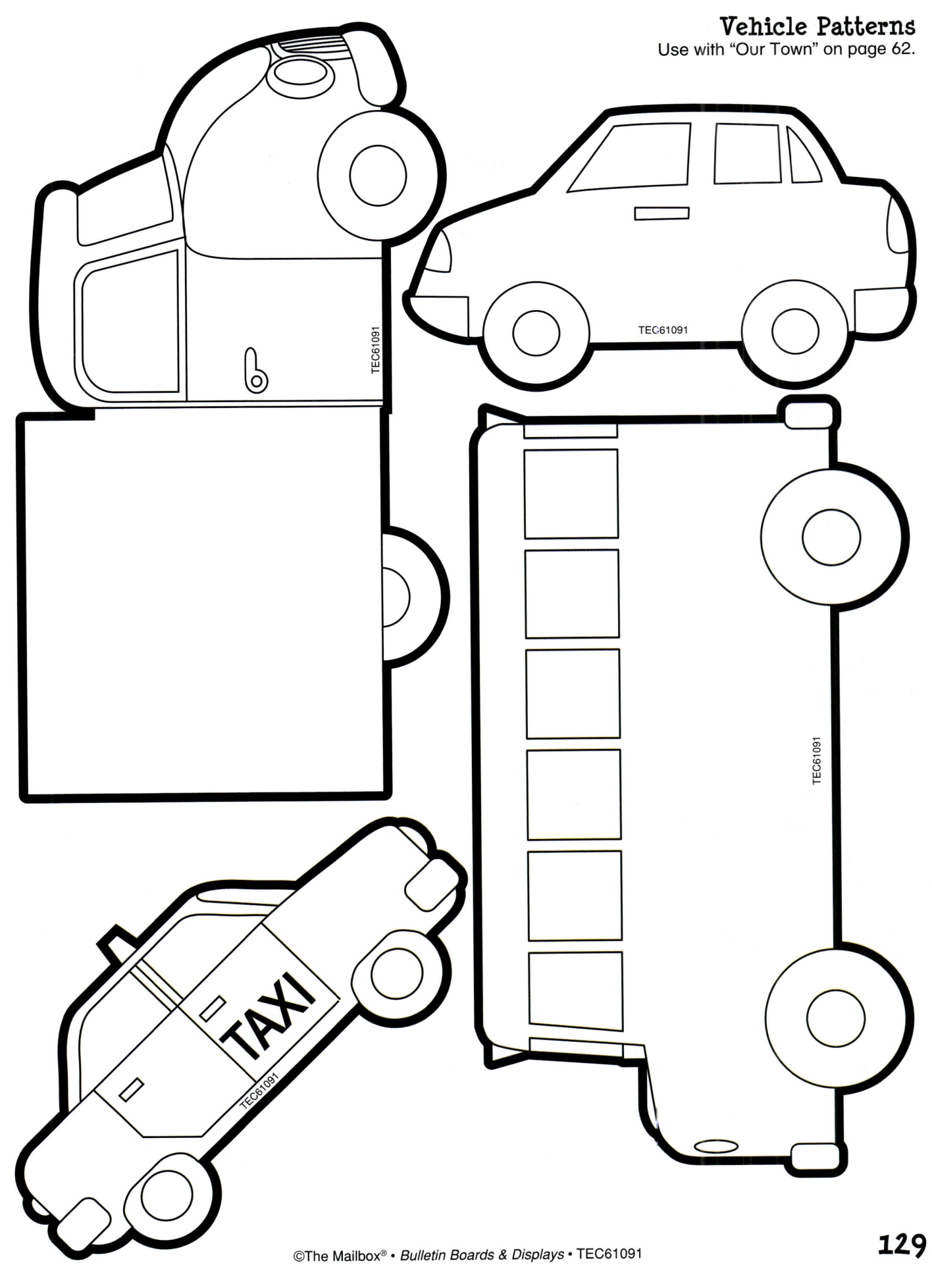

Vehicle Patterns
Use with "Our Town" on page 62.

129

Bear Pattern
Use with "Peekaboo Bears!" on page 62.

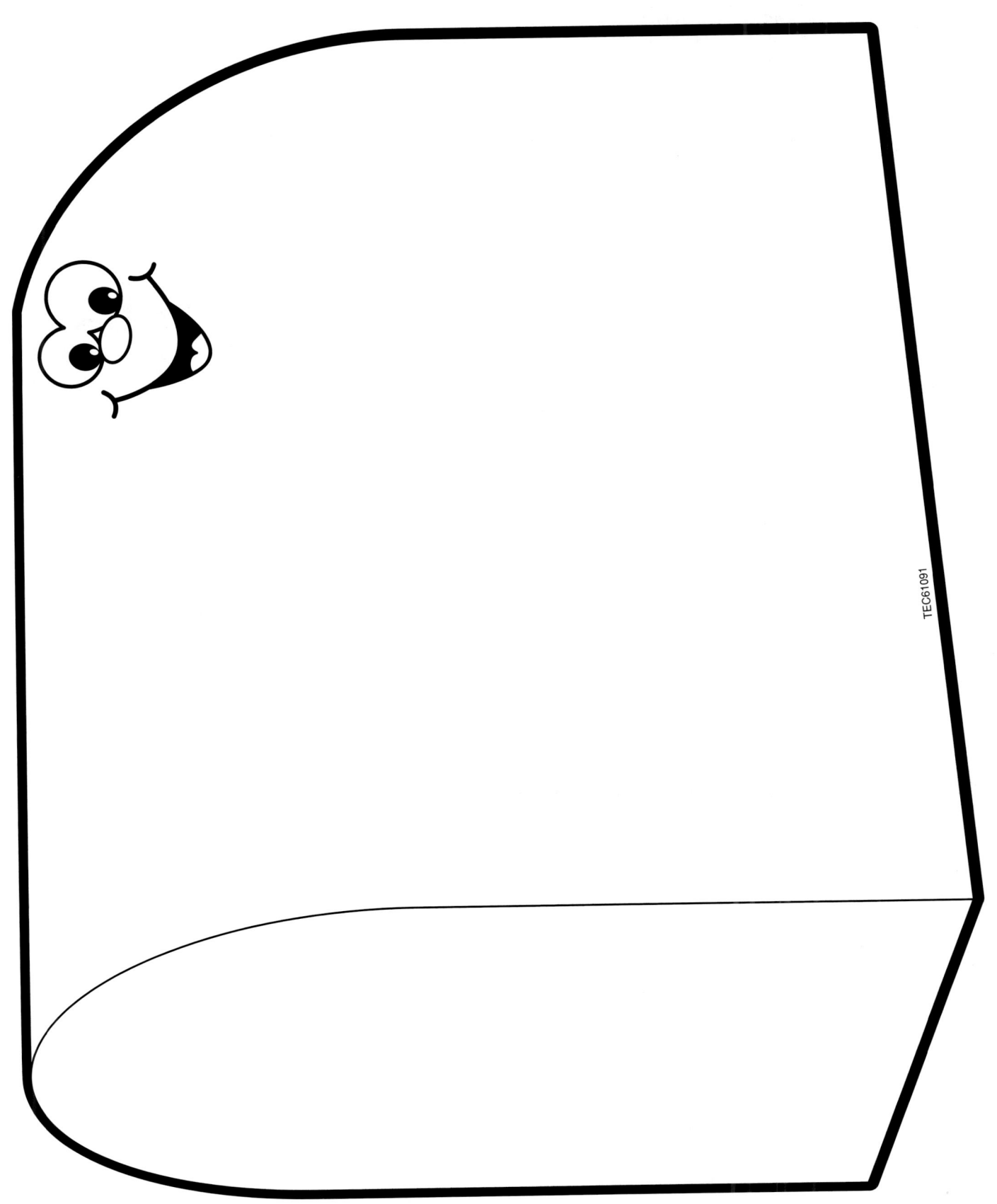

Mailbox Pattern
Use with "You've Got Mail!" on page 65.

Hat and Boot Patterns
Use with "Together Again!" on page 66.

Cookie Patterns
Use with "Freshly Baked!" on page 66.

Transportation Cards
Use with "I Spy Transportation!" on page 67.

135

Work Display Pattern
Use with "Our Work Is Bright!" on page 68.

Look at What I Did!

Tag Patterns
Use with "Handy Work!" on page 68.

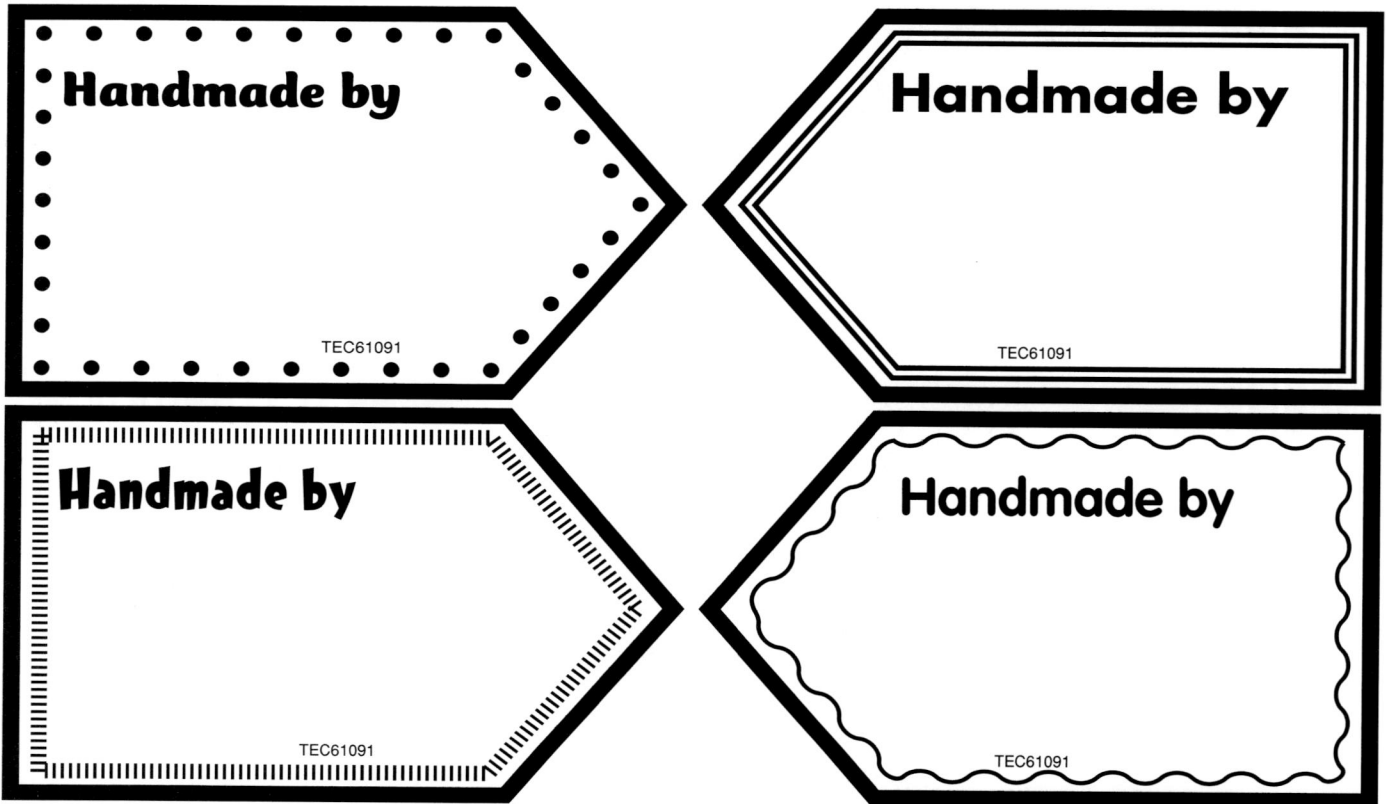

Star Patterns
Use with "Shining Stars!" on page 69.

Cat Pattern
Use with "Preschool Is 'Paws-itively' Terrific!" on page 70.

Rake, Hat, Watering Can, and Sunglasses Patterns
Use with the variations on page 70.

139

Gumball Machine Pattern
Use with "We Stick Together!" on page 71.

Elephant Pattern
Use with the display at the top of page 73.

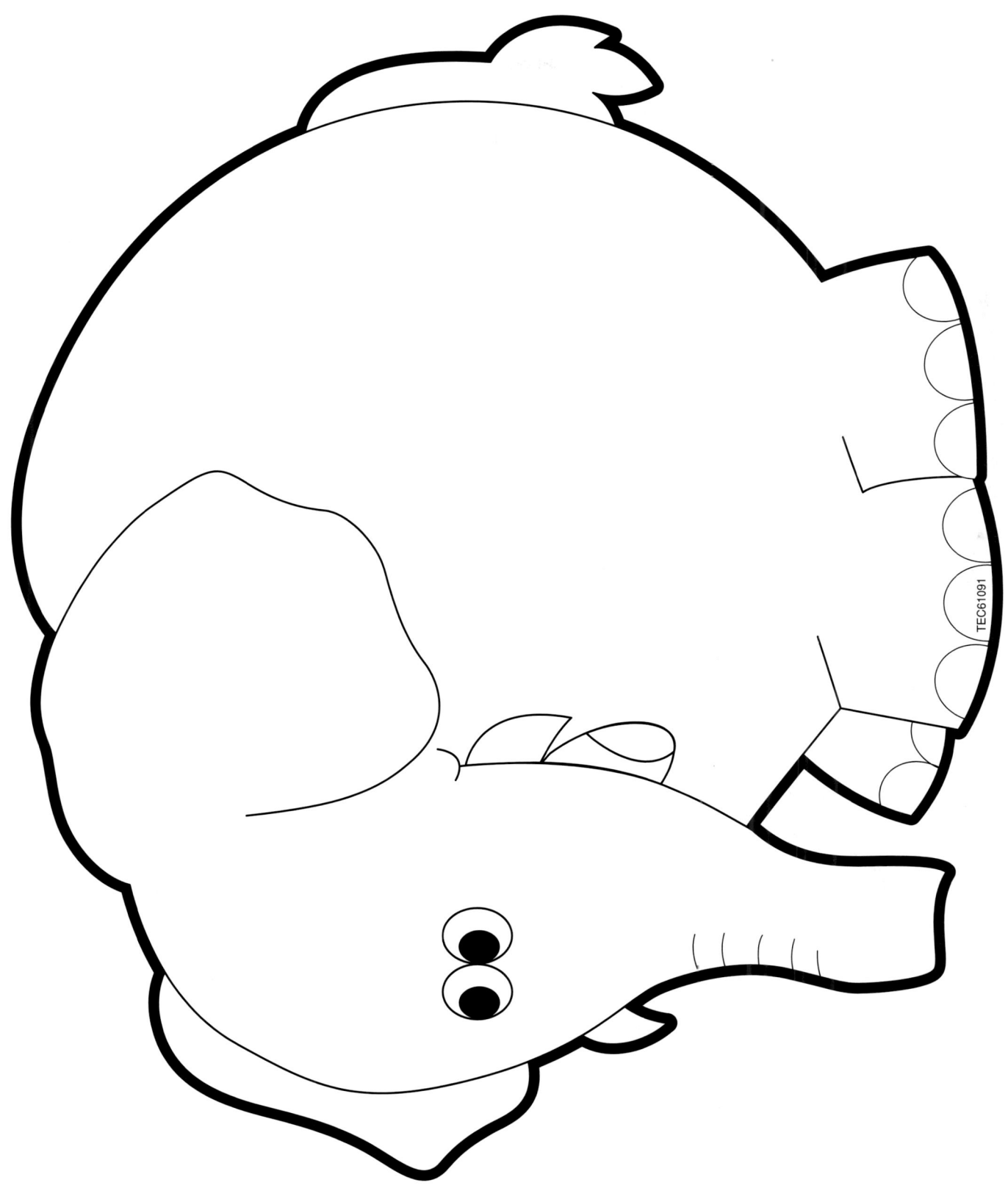

Index

acorns, 10, 17
ants, 60
apples, 15, 16
attendance, 72
balloons, 13
bears, 62
bees, 11, 16, 38, 48, 49
behavior, 48, 71
birds, 72
birthdays, 13
bubbles, 63
butterflies, 47
cat, 70
caterpillar, 71
Chicka Chicka Boom Boom, 64
Christmas, 27–29, 31
classroom jobs, 11, 12, 73
community, 62
compact discs, 6
cookie jar, 66
crayons, 5
crow, 18
dandelions, 53
dental health, 36
dogs, 19
Dr. Seuss, 39, 107
ducks, 11, 46
elephant, 73
families, 16, 22, 91
fire safety, 19
fish, 8, 46, 73
flowers, 16, 43, 49, 50
friends, 9

frogs, 46
gifts, 29
gingerbread cookies, 28
gingerbread house, 26
grapes, 7
Green Eggs and Ham, 39
Groundhog Day, 36
gumball machine, 71
gumdrops, 30
Halloween, 19–21
handprints, 12, 18, 19, 24, 27, 35, 43, 47, 52, 56, 68
Hanukkah, 27
harvest, 18
holiday lights, 27
holidays (see individual holidays)
hot-air balloons, 6
Humpty Dumpty, 66
hygiene, 63
ice cream, 59
interactive displays, 17, 30, 41, 43, 44, 45, 55, 62, 64–67, 71–73
kites, 12, 42
Kwanzaa, 31
ladybugs, 45
lambs, 41
leaves, 16, 17
leprechauns, 40
letters, 64, 65
lobster, 58
mail, 65
management
 anytime, 71–73

welcome to school, 11–14
Martin Luther King Jr. Day, 35
memories, 7, 51, 54, 59
mouse, 55, 66
mud, 44
mummy, 21
musical notes, 6
New Year's Day, 32, 33
ocean, 57, 58
octopus, 58
parental involvement, 14, 73
patriotic, 60
penguins, 33
picnic, 60
pig, 44
polar bear, 34
pond life, 46
Presidents' Day, 38
pumpkins, 20
puzzle, 8, 66
quilt, 61
racetrack, 54
rain, 43, 44
rainbow, 42, 43
raindrops, 44
reindeer, 28
sailboats, 52
sand castles, 57
scarecrow, 18
shamrocks, 40
snorkeling, 57
snowflakes, 16
snowpals, 35
spiders, 19
squirrel, 10, 17, 25
starfish, 58
stars, 13, 69
St. Patrick's Day, 40
strawberries, 55
student photographs, 6, 16, 20, 28, 36, 40, 49, 51, 53, 60
sun, 53, 68
supplies, 14
Thanksgiving, 22–24, 91
train, 31
transportation, 67
tree, 16, 22, 29, 64
turkeys, 23, 24
turtle, 46
Valentine's Day, 37, 38
watermelon, 56
welcome, 54
winter wear, 25, 32
wishing well, 14
work displays
   anytime, 68–70
   spring, 49
   welcome to school, 7

Pattern Index

A
acorn, 79
ant, 128
apple, 85

B
barn, 111
bear, 103, 130
bee and wings, 118
bees, 81
boots, 133
bows, 83
boxcar, 99

C
candy, 95
cat, 138
child, 77
cookies, 134
corn, 97
crayon, 74

D
dalmatian, 88
duck, 82, 116

E
egg and ham, 107
elephant, 141
engine, 98

F
feather, 92
fish, 76, 116
frog, 117

G
gingerbread cookies, 96
groundhog, 105
gumball machine, 140

H
hats, 102, 133, 139
hive, 80
hot-air balloon, 75
Humpty Dumpty, 132

I
ice cream scoop, 128

L
ladybug, 114
lamb head and feet, 110
leaves, 86
leprechaun, 109
lobster, 126
log, 115

M
mailbox, 131
mitten, 100
mouse, 123
musical notes, 75

P
pawprints, 104
penguin, 101
pig, 113
pumpkin, 89
puppy, 120

R
racecars, 122
raindrops, 112
rake, 139

S
sail and boat, 119
scarecrow, 87
shamrock, 108
skates, 102
snorkeler, 125
snowflakes, 86
sock, 100
squirrel, 78
starfish, 127
stars, 83, 137
strawberries, 124
sun, 121
sunglasses, 139

T
tags, 136
tooth and toothbrush, 106
transportation cards, 135
tree, 90
turkey, 93
turkey head and feet, 92
turtle head, legs, and tail, 117

V
vehicles, 129

W
watering can, 139
wings, 118
winter clothing, 94
wishing well, 84
work display, 136
worms, 85

Everyone's Talking About The MAILBOX® Books!

"Your books give hands-on, practical ideas. I love them!"

Tricia Dougherty—Grade 2
McNichols Plaza School
Scranton, PA

"I love all of your books!"

Deborah Hudspeth—Preschool
FBC Day School
Tupelo, MS

"I love the books I have bought from The Mailbox. They are easily aligned to the CA standards..."

DebraLee Reichard
Yucca Valley, CA

"I like the...wonderful ideas for reading, writing, and math."

Cynthia Oliver—Grade 3
Cedar Hills Elementary
Jacksonville, FL

"I absolutely LOVE books from The Mailbox. The ideas contained in each book are well thought-out and easily implemented in the classroom."

Linda Barnes—Preschool
Orange, CA

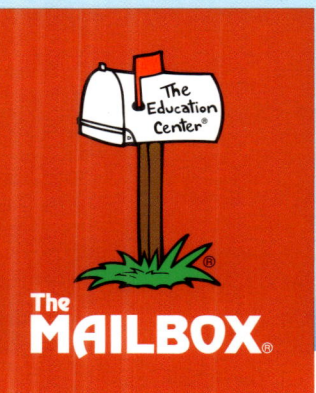

grade **PreK**

Bulletin Boards & Displays

The MAILBOX®
The Education Center®

TEC61091

Find just the display you need—the one that will capture kids' interest and showcase all they've learned—with *Bulletin Boards & Displays*. Whether you're looking for a fun kid-centered display, seasonal bulletin board, or classroom management tool, this book gives you a fresh supply of irresistible ideas for your classroom. With this book's simple directions and color illustrations, preparing bulletin boards, wall displays, and door decorations has never been easier. You'll get

- suggestions on how to create different displays using the same elements
- patterns for easy construction
- an index and a skills grid to help you quickly find the display you need
- handy storage tips

Also available from The Mailbox® Books:

TEC60801. Big Book of Patterns • Preschool–Kindergarten
TEC60816. The Best of *The Mailbox*® Bulletin Boards • Book 2 • Preschool–Kindergarten
TEC61046. *The Mailbox*® Superbook® • Preschool

www.themailbox.com

ISBN-13: 978-1562...
ISBN-10: 156234761...

TEACHER'S EDITION

LifePrints
ESL FOR ADULTS

2